Grade 3

Credits
Content Editor: Erin McCarthy
Copy Editor: Carrie Fox

Visit *carsondellosa.com* for correlations to Common Core, state, national, and Canadian provincial standards.

Carson-Dellosa Publishing LLC
PO Box 35665
Greensboro, NC 27425 USA
carsondellosa.com

ISBN 978-1-4838-3846-5
01-345177784

Table of Contents

What Is Math Workshop?

One of the most challenging aspects of teaching mathematics is differentiating instruction to meet the needs of all of the learners in your classroom. As a classroom teacher, you are responsible for teaching the standards that must be met by the end of the year. But, the reality inside the classroom is that one size does not fit all. For some students, the material is too difficult. For others, it is too easy.

With both reading and writing, many teachers have found the workshop model to be an excellent way to teach students at various levels. It allows for whole-group and small-group instruction, and individual practice so teachers can monitor students' progress and vary instruction according to need. The same workshop approach can be used for successful math instruction. This model encourages students to go beyond passive learning and become mathematicians who can think critically.

Like reading and writing workshops, math workshop is a structure, not a curriculum. It can be used with existing curriculums and materials and should be adapted to best fit the needs of the teacher and students. Math workshop will look different from classroom to classroom but usually includes the same building blocks: a warm-up, a whole-class mini-lesson, leveled small-group instruction, and individual practice. For a more in-depth look at the elements of math workshop, refer to pages 4 and 5.

Using a math workshop model allows teachers to:
- meet the needs of learners at all levels
- encourage deeper learning than in traditional lessons
- spiral concepts throughout the year
- work with any curriculum
- group students flexibly so they can move according to their changing needs
- offer repeated opportunities for practice
- keep students consistently engaged in learning

Starting math workshop in your classroom can seem overwhelming if you've never done it before. Use the guides on pages 4 through 14 to help you decide how math workshop will work in your classroom, plan your lessons, and manage the day-to-day details. Then, get started with over 25 preplanned lessons and activities. Use the blank reproducible activities starting on page 183 to create your own practice and review activities to be used throughout the year.

The Elements of Math Workshop

The major parts of math workshop are a warm-up, a mini-lesson, rotations (which include guided math groups, independent practice, and conferencing), and closure. You do not have to follow this format exactly. Instead, mix, match, and tweak things to make math workshop work for your classroom. See page 6 for more information on how math workshop can be changed to better fit your needs. Once you understand the basics, you can use the information below to plan your own math workshop lessons. Refer to pages 9 and 10 for more information on planning math workshop lessons.

1 Warm-Up
about 5 minutes

The warm-up is used to get students thinking mathematically and prepare them for the mini-lesson. It can be the same every day, or changed to relate to the lesson focus. You may choose to discuss only a portion of the assignment, such as a few sections of the calendar bulletin board or a single review problem.

Options*:
- number talks or number study
- problem of the day
- calendar time
- quick games (for example, Buzz or Around the World)
- discussion of an incorrectly solved problem
- number of the day (use the template on page 183)
- fact fluency practice
- daily review problems

2 Mini-Lesson
10–15 minutes

The mini-lesson is a teacher-led, whole-group activity. This is when new vocabulary and foundational information should be introduced and modeled. Teachers should model math thinking as they work through example problems. Often, students work with a practice problem to clear up any misconceptions.

Options*:
- present a textbook lesson
- show an introduction video
- solve a problem and think aloud
- demonstrate a new strategy
- direct a hands-on activity
- create an anchor chart
- share a math read-aloud
- review the previous day's lesson

*Please note that the options provided are a starting point and there are many more options you can explore for each section.

3 **Rotations**
10–20
minutes each

Students rotate through guided math with the teacher, independent practice, and workstations. This is also the time when teachers may choose to skip small group instruction in favor of one-on-one conferencing with students.

Guided Math

During this time, you work with small (eight or fewer students), flexible, leveled groups of students to extend and enhance the mini-lesson. Students use manipulatives to better understand the reasoning, procedures, strategies, etc., of the topic. Focus on using math talk and math tools to make sure students really understand the topic. Begin with the lowest group so they do not work on independent practice until after small-group instruction. Like the mini-lesson, these lessons can follow the warm-up/explanation/guided practice/independent practice/assessment model, although they don't have to.

Independent Stations

This segment is also known as centers, rotations, workstations, etc. Activities can be individual, partner, or small group and often include both practice of the current skill or topic and review of past skills. Activities should be introduced ahead of time so students can work independently and should be at a level that won't produce frustration. Students can follow a strict rotation or may be given daily choices as long as they complete certain set activities each week.

Options*:
- math games and activities
- fact fluency practice
- Solve the Room activities
- technology centers (including online games and district-mandated math programs)

- practice sheets (*Note:* The practice sheets included in the lessons are all different, so students can progress through them as they gain understanding of the skill.)
- journaling and/or interactive notebooks

Conferencing

Instead of leading guided math groups, you may choose to periodically observe students during independent stations or pull students for one-on-one conferencing. This allows for formative assessment and more targeted instruction for students who need more help with a skill. This is also an ideal time to do state- or district-mandated quarterly testing.

4 **Closure/ Reflection**
3–5
minutes

The closure is a short, targeted way to wrap up the learning students did during math workshop. It is the perfect time to review the math objective or essential question and answer any questions students may still have.

Options*:
- exit tickets
- allow a few students to explain an "ah-ha!" moment they had
- think/pair/share problem-solving
- math talk prompts

- quick journaling
- students can share what they learned in their own words
- Q and A time

*Please note that the options provided are a starting point and there are many more options you can explore for each section.

What Does Math Workshop Look Like?

Due to the nature of the workshop model, math workshop will look different in different classrooms. You can change it however you need so that it works best for your classroom. See below for ideas and examples of how you can reshape math workshop for your needs.

Timing and Structure
- You can conduct math workshop daily, a few times a week, or monthly.
- Or, you can use one or two days to teach longer whole-class lessons and use the remaining days for rotations.
- Meet with each leveled group daily, or only once or twice a week, depending on how long your math block is.
- Have students visit every station daily or visit each station once each week.

Content
- Use your textbook, a prescribed curriculum, or make your own lessons.
- You can have students use math notebooks for recording work and/or journaling.
- Use the same handful of simple games so you don't have to reinvent the wheel (for example, sorting activities, puzzles, concentration, etc.).
- The lessons provided in this book are interchangeable. If you don't like one or more of the suggestions, replace it with your own.

Assessment
- Build in formal assessment as a longer closure, as a station to visit, or take a day off to administer a test.
- You may choose to have students record the results from each activity or use a checklist during rotations.
- See page 13 for more information on accountability during math workshop.

Grouping
- Groups do not have to be the same size.
- You can have more than one group at the same level to ensure small groups.
- To group students, you can use formative assessment, pretests, or group them on the fly after observations made during the previous day or the mini-lesson.
- You can choose to move students between leveled groups as needed (which could even mean daily) or after more formal assessments.

Choice
- You can require students to visit rotations in a certain order and/or on specific days.
- Or, you can allow students to choose which centers to complete each day.
- You may choose to make students responsible for completing all of the rotations by the end of the week, or you can make some rotations mandatory each day (such as independent practice, fact fluency, and technology centers).
- Students can complete rotations at their desks so you can keep an eye on them, or you can allow them to work in various spots around the room.

Managing Math Workshop

Math workshop can be daunting to newcomers because of all of the elements that need preparation and upkeep. However, the tips and suggestions below for managing the various parts of math workshop will help you get started on the right foot and maintain it throughout the year.

Starting and Maintaining Math Workshop

- Set student expectations before beginning. See page 11 for more information.
- Don't underestimate the power of positive reinforcement.
- Stop and practice the routines and procedures as needed throughout the year if students aren't following expectations.
- Start slow! Begin with only one game or activity during rotations.
- Practice any new games or activities with the whole group first.
- Keep it simple. To begin with, use familiar activities such as concentration, war, or dominoes.
- As you introduce new activities through the year, use the same formats so you don't have to teach a new set of rules each time.
- If possible, use assistants or parent volunteers to monitor students during the first few weeks.
- During weeks with field trips, assemblies, etc., try to move math workshop to a different time. Or, use the entire week to review old concepts and meet with groups that need more help with old concepts instead of introducing a new topic.

Organizing Materials

- Keep all of the necessary supplies in the area where you meet for guided math. That way, students don't waste time looking for materials such as pencils, paper, and manipulatives.
- Use bins or baskets to organize activities, games, and small group supplies for guided math, so everything needed to complete the activity is in one easy-to-grab place.
- Make all math manipulatives visible and accessible so students can use whatever tools they need whenever they need to.
- Make several copies of each activity so multiple pairs or groups of students can work on the same one.
- Designate a student or students each week to be the Materials Master. Their job is to make sure all materials are cleaned up and organized each day.

Managing Math Workshop, cont.

Classroom Management

Managing Rotations

- Use a bulletin board, pocket chart, or interactive whiteboard for a visual reminder of the rotations order. Refer to the example below.
- Use sticky notes with student names to make reorganizing leveled groups quick and easy.
- Use visual cues and directions on games so students can work independently.
- When students are absent, you can catch them up during conferencing/one-on-one time or temporarily move them to a lower group.

Student Behavior

- For early finishers: have review, extension, or older activities available; make a packet with word problems or challenges to complete; or create a chart listing things they can move on to.
- Foster independence with an "ask three before me" policy.
- Have students use a special hand signal so they can ask to use the bathroom without interrupting guided math.
- For students who have trouble working independently, remove them from rotations and have them sit at a desk near the guided math group until they are ready to rejoin rotations. It may be helpful to have those students start back slowly, with only one independent activity reintroduced at a time.

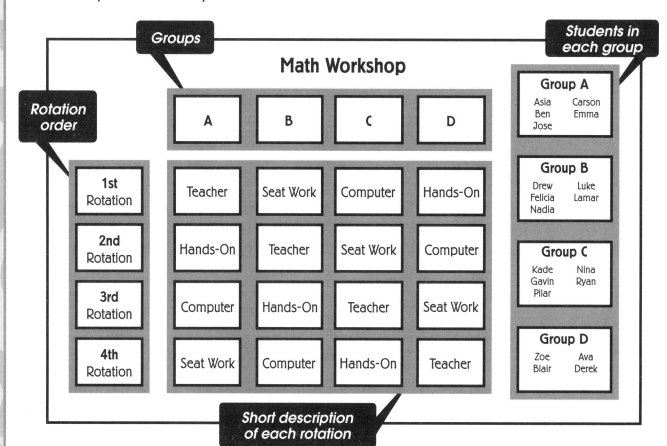

Planning and Preparation

As with anything, math workshop will be less stressful and have a better chance of success if you plan in advance. Use your district's scope and sequence, textbook curriculum, or similar to plan roughly when and how long to teach each topic. Then, plan the specifics for only a week or two at a time to allow room for remediation or moving on early, depending on what students need. Use the reproducible below to create a high-level plan for a week. Use page 10 to plan more specifically for the guided math groups for that week.

Math Workshop

Week of _____

Objective:	Essential Question:

Mini-Lesson		Rotations
Monday		
Tuesday		
Wednesday		
Thursday		
Friday		

Guided Math

Week of _____

Group 1	Level:	Group 2	Level:
Students:		Students:	

Group 3	Level:	Group 4	Level:
Students:		Students:	

	Group 1	Group 2	Group 3	Group 4
Monday				
Tuesday				
Wednesday				
Thursday				
Friday				

Student Expectations

Math workshop will not be perfect from the start. It may be a bit chaotic and students may try to play instead of work. But, by setting student expectations early, and with plenty of practice and modeling, math workshop can run smoothly.

Questions to Consider

How should materials be handled? Will there be dedicated students in charge of the materials? Where will they be stored? When can students access them? How and when should cleanup happen? Should there be a one-minute cleanup warning before switching rotations or is cleaning up part of the transition time? Who is responsible for cleaning up common areas?

How and when can students work with others? What activities should be done alone, with a partner, or as group work? Who and when can students ask for help?

What does staying on task mean in math workshop? What level should the volume be? Where should students be working? How should students be accountable for the work they've done? What should the conversations sound like?

What happens if students make mistakes or struggle? Who can they ask for help? What materials and strategies are available if a problem is too hard? Can they skip difficult problems or save them for conferencing?

When is the teacher available? Can students interrupt guided math groups? How can they signal they need to go to the bathroom? What is an appropriate reason to interrupt the teacher? Who else can help students and answer questions?

Setting Expectations

One of the first things you should do when beginning math workshop is to clearly outline the expectations. While you don't have to do this in tandem with making an anchor chart, the visual reminder can be helpful for retaining the expectations as well as serving as a visual reminder throughout the year.

- It can be helpful to frame the expectations simply: What should math workshop look like? What should it sound like? What is the student responsible for? What is the teacher responsible for? Refer to the Questions to Consider in the section above for more specific things to discuss.
- Use the reproducible provided on page 12 for students to complete and keep in their math notebooks or folders. Or, have students and parents sign it as a behavior contract at the beginning of the year. It may be helpful to preprogram the information before copying for students who need it.
- Review the anchor chart often in the first few weeks. Start reviewing it daily before beginning math workshop, and then gradually review it less often as students become more self-reliant.

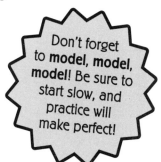
Don't forget to **model, model, model!** Be sure to start slow, and practice will make perfect!

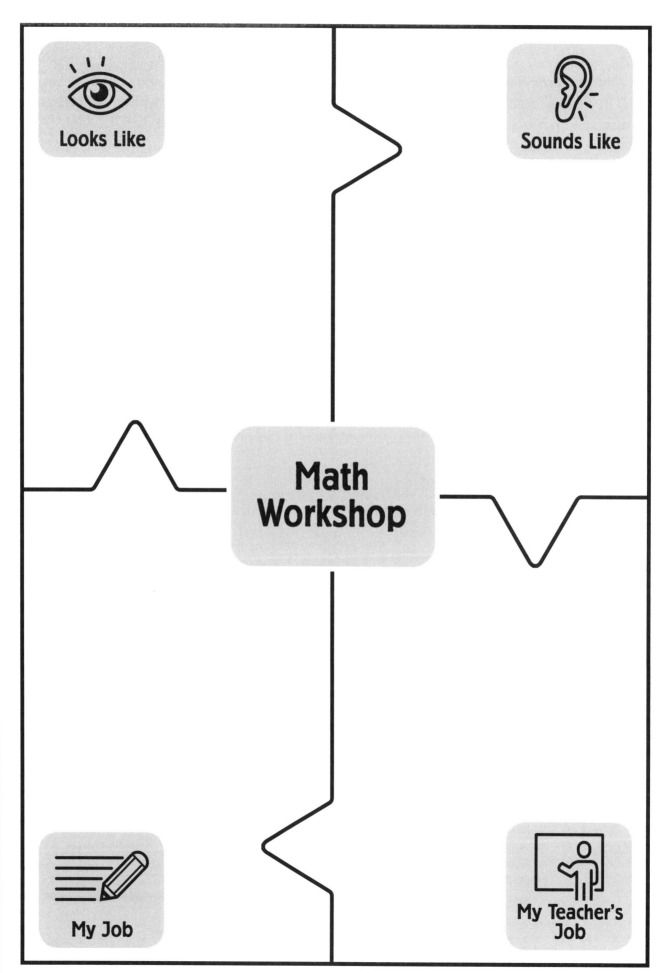

Looks Like

Sounds Like

Math Workshop

My Job

My Teacher's Job

Ensuring Accountability

While moving to a math workshop model has many benefits, it removes the traditional assessment and accountability options in the traditional teaching model. However, it's still necessary to prove in some way that students are working hard toward learning goals and making progress throughout the year. See the lists below for suggestions.

Accountability During Rotations

- Have students record their math thinking (for example, number sentences solved during a game) on whiteboards or something else that is highly visible. That way, you can see at a glance if students are working or not.
- Use activities with recording sheets that you can collect.
- Or, use a recording sheet where students record the rotations they visited and details about their work at each rotation.
- If desired, collect students' written work and/or recording sheets for a participation grade. Use the reproducible on page 14 as a weekly rotation recording sheet or create your own with the rotations specific to your math workshop (see example below).
- Initial, stamp, or sticker students' work daily. You can circulate and do this quickly during closure each day.
- Have students use a math journal to record their work during rotations.
- Utilize technology if possible—many programs and apps have built-in reports on the teacher side.

Assessment

- When not meeting with groups, use the guided math time to visit different stations and have students explain their math thinking for a quick formative assessment.
- During closure, use exit tickets. Use them as formative assessments, or keep them in a math notebook or portfolio to show progress.
- Designate one math workshop day a week or month for a more formal assessment that can be used for a grade or kept in portfolios.

Name_____   Date _____

Math Workshop

Mark off each rotation as you complete it. You must do seat work and technology every day!

Mon	Meet with Teacher	Seat Work	Technology	Fast Practice	Math Game
Tues	Meet with Teacher	Seat Work	Technology	Fast Practice	Math Game
Wed	Meet with Teacher	Seat Work	Technology	Fast Practice	Math Game

Name _____   Week of _____

Math Rotations

Day	Rotation(s) Visited	Done?	Rate Yourself
Monday			
Tuesday			
Wednesday			
Thursday			
Friday			

1	2	3	4
I didn't do any work. I wasn't on task.	I didn't do my best work and was often off task.	I worked well, but was off task a little.	I worked hard and stayed on task.

Understanding Multiplication

 Essential Question

How can the products of whole numbers be expressed?

 Warm-Up/Review

Write or display a repeated addition problem on the board, such as *25 + 25 + 25 = ?* and have students solve it with a partner and share their answers. Challenge students to think of another way to solve the problem using a different operation. Discuss students' ideas as a class.

 Mini-Lesson

Materials: counters or square tiles, 1–9 number cards or tiles

1. Write *5 × 4* on the board. Ask, "What would this look like as an array?" Have students model the array using counters or square tiles. Then, have students share the repeated addition sentence with a partner. Record it on the board.

2. Demonstrate skip counting by 5s to find the product. Add *= 20* to the multiplication sentence. Then, label and define the factors and product. Explain, "Factors are the numbers you multiply together. The product is the answer to a multiplication sentence."

3. Repeat with several more multiplication problems with factors less than 10. Emphasize the repeated addition and skip counting and encourage students to use the correct vocabulary.

4. Say, "Multiplication facts are very helpful to know, because it can take a lot of time to add or skip count to find each product. That is why it is useful to memorize the products."

5. Display a multiplication chart and challenge students to look for patterns in the products for each factor. For example, *all products of 2 are even numbers, all products of 5 end in 5 or 0, the products of 4 are the same as every other product of 2*, etc.

6. Have students work with a partner to draw two number cards and write the multiplication sentence, the repeated addition sentence, and then solve. Students should create arrays as needed to find the products.

 Math Talk

Can you solve this problem using another strategy? How?
How is multiplication related to addition?
Do you notice any patterns in this factor and its products?

 Journal Prompt

Explain why it is useful to memorize multiplication facts.

Materials

counters
laminated place value mats
dry-erase markers

 Workstations

Activity sheets (pages 17–19)
Multiplication Speedway
   (page 20)
Multiplication facts flash cards

 Guided Math

○ **Remediation: Using Counters to Multiply**

1. Write *8 × 3*. Provide students with counters. Say, "How can you use the counters to help solve this problem?" Create 3 separate groups with 8 counters in each group. Say the addition problem *8 + 8 + 8* while pointing to the 3 groups. Explain that multiplication is a shorter way to represent repeated addition.

2. Now, write *9 × 5*. Have students use counters to solve the problem and write the addition problems that they used to solve the problem.

3. Have students continue practicing with multi-digit numbers less than 10.

☐ **On Level: The Commutative Property**

1. Write *3 × 6*. Ask students to use their own methods to solve the problem. Then, have students share the steps they took to solve the problem.

2. Explain, "Like in addition, you can switch the order of the factors and the answer stays the same." Model a 3 × 6 array with counters. Then, move the same counters to create a 6 × 3 array. Emphasize how the same exact amount of counters was used to create each array, and the factors just switched places.

3. Display the following problems: *4 × 7, 2 × 8,* and *3 × 9*. Have students create both arrays, record both multiplication sentences, and solve each problem.

4. Say, "You don't have to memorize all of the multiplication facts. Once you know one fact, like *4 × 7,* you know the turnaround fact also."

△ **Enrichment: Working with Larger Numbers**

1. Write *12 × 5*. Have students record *12* on their place value mats.

2. Say, "We can divide larger numbers into place values and multiply each place by the single factor." Have students record each operation and product on their mat as you explain. Say, "12 is 10 + 2. 10 × 5 is 50. 2 × 5 is 10. I can add those products together to get the final product: 50 + 10 is 60."

3. Repeat with several more 2-digit by 1-digit problems. Encourage students to use place value to break up each 2-digit number before multiplying. Have students share their answers and strategies.

 Assess and Extend

Have students solve the following problem: *At the store, popcorn comes in boxes with 6 bags of popcorn each. Lucy bought 6 boxes to bring to a party. How many bags of popcorn will Lucy bring to the party?*

16

Understanding Multiplication ● Using Counters to Multiply

Add. Then, multiply.

---

1. ☆☆ ☆☆

  ☆☆ ☆☆

_____ + _____ + _____ + _____ = _____

_____ sets of _____ equals _____

_____ × _____ = _____

2.

_____ + _____ + _____ = _____

_____ sets of _____ equals _____

_____ × _____ = _____

3.

_____ + _____ + _____ + _____

+ _____ = _____

_____ sets of _____ equals _____

_____ × _____ = _____

---

4. ☆ ☆ ☆ ☆ ☆ ☆

  ☆ ☆ ☆ ☆ ☆ ☆

  ☆ ☆ ☆ ☆ ☆ ☆

_____ + _____ + _____ + _____ + _____

+ _____ = _____

_____ sets of _____ equals _____

_____ × _____ = _____

Draw pictures to show each problem. Then, fill in the blanks.

5.

2 sets of 3 equals _____

_____ + _____ = _____

_____ × _____ = _____

6.

4 sets of 5 equals _____

_____ + _____ + _____ + _____ = _____

_____ × _____ = _____

Understanding Multiplication ☐ The Commutative Property

Shuffle several sets of 0–9 number cards. Choose two cards. Use the numbers to complete the sentence. Draw both arrays. Then, write both related multiplication facts and solve.

1. I chose a _____ and a _____ .

_____

_____

2. I chose a _____ and a _____ .

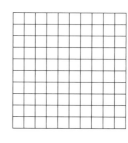

_____

_____

3. I chose a _____ and a _____ .

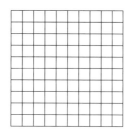

_____

_____

4. I chose a _____ and a _____ .

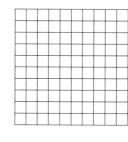

_____

_____

5. I chose a _____ and a _____ .

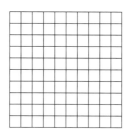

_____

_____

6. I chose a _____ and a _____ .

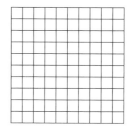

_____

_____

Name _____   Date _____

Write the repeated addition problem for each equation. Then, solve. Show your work with numbers or drawings.

1. $10 \times 2 =$ _____

_____

2. $15 \times 4 =$ _____

_____

3. $12 \times 2 =$ _____

_____

4. $14 \times 3 =$ _____

_____

5. $10 \times 6 =$ _____

_____

6. $11 \times 3 =$ _____

_____

7. $13 \times 4 =$ _____

_____

8. $16 \times 0 =$ _____

_____

9. $20 \times 4 =$ _____

_____

10. $12 \times 5 =$ _____

_____

11. $10 \times 5 =$ _____

_____

12. $13 \times 2 =$ _____

_____

13. $14 \times 1 =$ _____

_____

14. $11 \times 2 =$ _____

_____

Multiplication Speedway

Materials: 1 die, multiplication facts flash cards, 1 counter per player

To play: Shuffle the multiplication fact cards and place in a pile facedown. Players take turns. Draw a card and answer the problem. If you are correct, roll the die and move forward that many spaces. If not, lose a turn. The first player to reach the Finish space wins.

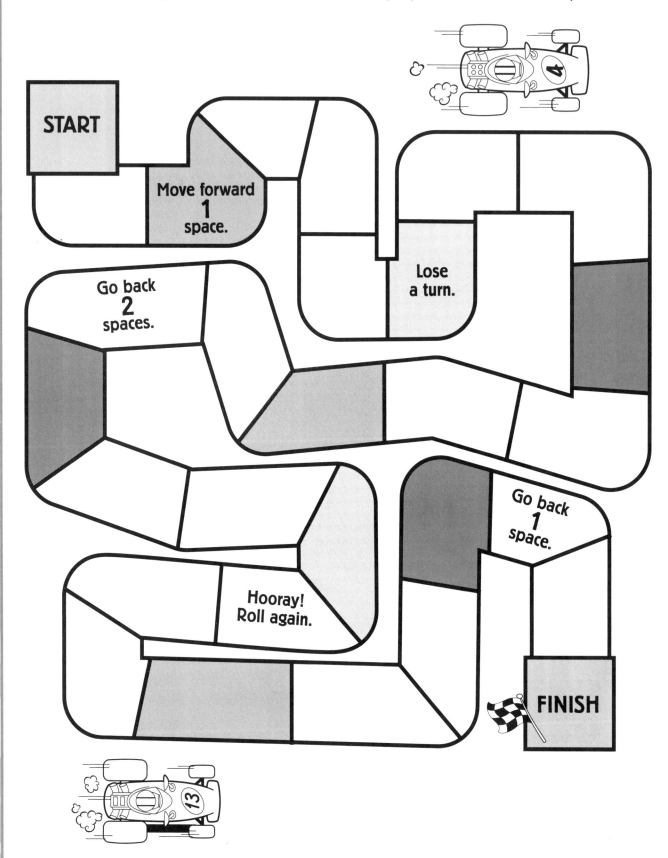

START

Move forward
1
space.

Go back
2
spaces.

Lose
a turn.

Go back
1
space.

Hooray!
Roll again.

FINISH

Understanding Division

 Essential Question

How can a set of objects be divided equally?

Warm-Up/Review

Discuss with students a time when they had to share a large amount of something. For example, a batch of cookies with their family, or a bag of balls with their classmates at recess. Challenge them to explain how they decided how many each person got.

 Mini-Lesson

Materials: counters, dry-erase markers and boards

1. Give each student 12 counters. Explain that there are 12 marshmallows and 6 friends. How can the marshmallows be divided so that each friend has the same amount?

2. Draw 6 stick figures on the board and have students draw 6 stick figures on their dry-erase boards. Give each stick figure a counter as you say, "One for you, one for you," and so on. Have students use their counters to follow along.

3. After each stick figure has 1 counter, some counters are left over. Ask, "What should I do with the rest of the counters?" Give each stick figure a second counter. Then, point out that each stick figure has 2 counters. There are no leftover counters, or *remainders*.

4. Write the equation $12 \div 6 = 2$ on the board. Explain, "There were 12 marshmallows divided among 6 friends. Each of the 6 friends got 2 marshmallows. There are none left over. Twelve divided by 6 equals 2."

5. Continue practicing with other simple numbers that divide evenly.

 Math Talk

Explain how multiplication facts can help you solve this problem.
Is there another way that you could solve this problem? Explain.
What words told you to divide?

 Journal Prompt

Joey says $15 \div 2 = 7$. Is he correct? How do you know?

Materials

counters

 Workstations

Activity sheets (pages 23–25)
Race to the Top (page 26)
Multiplication Speedway
(page 20)
Multiplication and division facts
flash cards

 Guided Math

Remediation: Making Equal Groups

1. Place counters within students' reach. Write *24 ÷ 4*.
2. Point to the 24. Say, "This number tells us how many to start with." Ask students to take 24 counters. Then, point to the 4. Say, "This number tells us how many groups to make." Have students draw 4 large circles. Demonstrate how to place the counters one at a time, dividing them evenly between the 4 groups. Explain, "The answer, or the quotient, tells us how many are in each equal group. What is the quotient?" Read the complete equation together: "24 divided by 4 equals 6."
3. Ask, "What would happen if I had counters left over? Can I just make one group bigger? If I divided cookies between friends, would it be fair to give one person more than the others?" Explain that when you divide, each group must be equal.
4. Have students continue practicing with other numbers that can be evenly divided.

On Level: Relating Division and Multiplication

1. Write *5 + 3 = 8* and *8 – 3 = 5*. Discuss how addition and subtraction are inverse operations.
2. Next, write *36 ÷ 6*. Ask, "How can this problem be solved with a relationship similar to that of addition and subtraction? What do we know about the relationship between multiplication and division?" Explain that multiplication and division are also inverse operations.
3. Write *6 × _____ = 36*. Ask, "What times 6 equals 36? Thirty-six divided into 6 groups equals 6 in each group." Use the counters in an array to demonstrate 6 rows of 6 to confirm the solution.
4. Have students continue with other numbers, practicing using the relationship between multiplication and division.

Enrichment: Input and Output

1. Draw a T-chart. Write the following numbers on the left side: *56, 21, 14, 35*. Write the following numbers on the right side: *8, 3, 2, 5*.
2. Explain that this is an input/output chart. "When 56 is put in the chart, 8 comes out. When 21 is put in the chart, 3 comes out. What rule is applied to 56 and 21?" Emphasize that the rule has to be true for every number.
3. Discuss the strategies that students used to figure out that the rule is *÷7*.
4. Continue with a new chart. Write *27, 54, 36, and 18* on the left and *3, 6, 4, and 2* on the right. (*÷9*) Then, work with charts that have one or more numbers missing. Have students figure out the rule and what is missing. For example, write *12, 27, 30* and _____ on the left and write *4, _____, 10, and 5* on the right. (*÷3, 15, 9*)

 Assess and Extend

Have students solve the following problem: *Benjamin has 20 photos. He would like to arrange them in a rectangle to fit on the wall above his bed. How many rows and columns would make the best arrangement? Is there another configuration Benjamin can make? If so, what is it?*

Understanding Division ● Making Equal Groups

Draw a picture to match the division problem. Then, write the division problem. Solve.

1. Twelve divided into three sets equals _____.	**2.** Eight divided into four sets equals _____.
3. Twenty-four divided into three sets equals _____.	**4.** Twelve divided into four sets equals _____.
5. Nine divided into three sets equals _____.	**6.** Five divided into one set equals _____.
7. Ten divided into five sets equals _____.	**8.** Twenty-five divided into five sets equals _____.
9. Twelve divided into six sets equals _____.	**10.** Sixteen divided into four sets equals _____.

Understanding Division ■ Relating Division and Multiplication

Solve each division problem. Then, complete the multiplication problem that relates to the division problem. Show your work with numbers or drawings.

I. $72 \div 8 =$ _____ $8 \times$ _____ $= 72$ **2.** $54 \div 9 =$ _____ $9 \times$ _____ $= 54$

3. $16 \div 4 =$ _____ $4 \times$ _____ $= 16$ **4.** $18 \div 2 =$ _____ $2 \times$ _____ $= 18$

5. $48 \div 6 =$ _____ $6 \times$ _____ $= 48$ **6.** $63 \div 7 =$ _____ $7 \times$ _____ $= 63$

7. $36 \div 9 =$ _____ $9 \times$ _____ $= 36$ **8.** $40 \div 10 =$ _____ $10 \times$ _____ $= 40$

9. $15 \div 3 =$ _____ $3 \times$ _____ $= 15$ **10.** $32 \div 8 =$ _____ $8 \times$ _____ $= 32$

II. $25 \div 5 =$ _____ $5 \times$ _____ $= 25$ **12.** $27 \div 3 =$ _____ $3 \times$ _____ $= 27$

13. $24 \div 4 =$ _____ $4 \times$ _____ $= 24$ **14.** $40 \div 8 =$ _____ $8 \times$ _____ $= 40$

Understanding Division   ▲ Input and Output

Find the rule for each chart. Fill in any missing numbers. For problems 7 and 8, create your own input/output charts.

I. The rule is: _____

90	9
30	3
70	7
40	4

2. The rule is: _____

45	9
60	12
30	___
___	4

3. The rule is: _____

12	6
8	4
16	___
___	5

4. The rule is: _____

24	___
15	5
___	9
12	4

5. The rule is: _____

42	6
35	___
49	7
___	8

6. The rule is: _____

44	11
48	___
16	4
___	9

7. The rule is: _____

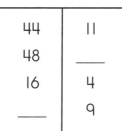

8. The rule is: _____

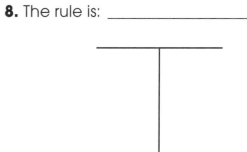

Race to the Top

Materials: 3 × 5 index cards with prepared division facts, crayons

To play: Players take turns. Choose a card. Find the quotient. If you are correct, color one space on the playing board. If you are not correct, you lose your turn. The first player to reach the tree wins the game.

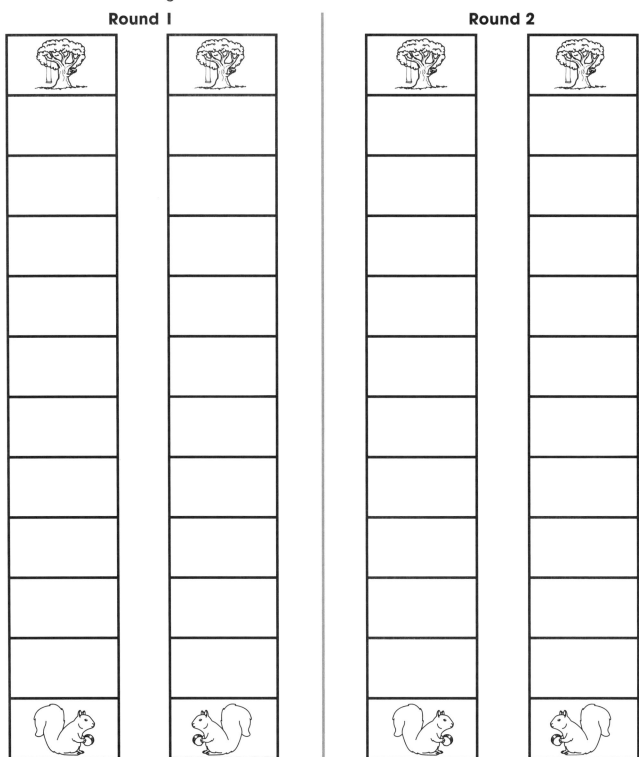

Round 1   Round 2

To prep: Write division facts on 3 × 5 index cards. Focus on specific facts that the class is working on, or write all facts for 0–9. Laminate the game board and fact cards. Place game board, division fact cards, and other materials in a center.

Relating Multiplication and Division

 Essential Question

How can understanding multiplication help to solve division problems?

 Warm-Up/Review

Write *5 + 3 = 8* on the board. Challenge students to write a related subtraction fact (*8 – 3 = 5 or 8 – 5 = 3*). Explain that just like addition and subtraction are related, and understanding both can help you solve the other, multiplication and division are also related.

 Mini-Lesson

1. Write *24 ÷ 8 = _____* on the board. Say, "How can you think about this as a multiplication problem? Whatever the unknown number is, if you multiply it by 8 you should get 24. So, what times 8 is 24? We know 8 × 3 = 24, so 24 ÷ 8 equals 3."

2. Write *24 ÷ 3 = _____* on the board. Say, "We also know 24 divided by 3 is going to be 8 because 3 × 8 = 24."

3. Write *48 ÷ _____ = 6* on the board. "One way to rephrase this is *6 times what is equal to 48*? We know 6 times 8 is equal to 48. So, 48 divided by 8 is equal to 6."

4. Have students practice with other problems: _____ ÷ 9 = 2, 12 ÷ _____ = 3, 56 ÷ _____ = 8, _____ ÷ 3 = 6, 30 ÷ _____ = 3. Students should give the related multiplication sentence that they used to solve for the missing number.

 Math Talk

How does knowing your multiplication facts make solving division problems easier?
Explain which problems are easier to solve and why (missing divisor, dividend, or quotient).
What related fact helped you solve this?

 Journal Prompt

Explain how you would solve 81 ÷ _____ = 9.

Materials

laminated multiplication charts
dry-erase markers

 Workstations

Activity sheets (pages 29–31)
Division Poke Cards (page 32)
Multiplication and division flash
cards

 Guided Math

⚪ **Remediation: Using a Multiplication Chart**

1. Write $18 \div 6 =$ _____ .
2. "How can you think about this as a multiplication problem? What number times 6 is 18? Look at your multiplication chart to help you." Model how to find the multiplication fact $6 \times 3 = 18$ in the chart by looking at the ×6 row or column, circling the 18, and following the other row or column to the left or top to find the other factor, 3. Write $6 \times 3 = 18$ below $18 \div 6 =$ _____ , pointing out how both equations use the same numbers.
3. Continue practicing using the multiplication chart with similar problems.

⬜ **On Level: Find the Missing Number**

1. Write _____ $\div 8 = 5$.
2. Ask, "How can you use multiplication to help you solve this problem? One way is to think, *8 times 5 equals what? I know 8 times 5 equals 40, therefore 40 divided by 8 equals 5.*"
3. Challenge students to write another division fact, using the same numbers, that is different from the one given. ($40 \div 5 = 8$)
4. Continue practicing with similar problems, varying where the missing number is in the division problem. Encourage students to rephrase each problem before solving.

🔺 **Enrichment: Fact Families**

1. Ask students to write a division problem of their choosing.
2. Write the problems in a column, one on top of the other. Review the vocabulary words for *dividend*, *divisor*, and *quotient*.
3. Next, ask students to write a multiplication problem that is related to the division problem they wrote. List those problems and discuss the words *factors* and *product*.
4. Have students write one more division problem and one more multiplication problem using the same numbers they used the first time. Discuss the term *fact family*.
5. Challenge students to write three more fact families and all the related division and multiplication problems, then share with the group.

 Assess and Extend

Have students solve the following problem: *Shanette has 41 erasers, and Zoe gives her 7 more. Shanette gives each of her 8 friends an equal number of erasers. How many erasers does each friend get?* (6)

Relating Multiplication and Division ● Using a Multiplication Chart

Use what you know about multiplication, or use a multiplication chart to find each quotient. Write the related multiplication sentence below each problem. The first one has been done for you.

1. $12 \div 6 = \boxed{2}$

$\mathbf{6 \times 2 = 12}$

2. $24 \div 4 = \boxed{}$

3. $40 \div 5 = \boxed{}$

4. $36 \div 6 = \boxed{}$

5. $72 \div 9 = \boxed{}$

6. $10 \div 2 = \boxed{}$

7. $36 \div 4 = \boxed{}$

8. $24 \div 8 = \boxed{}$

9. $20 \div 4 = \boxed{}$

10. $35 \div 7 = \boxed{}$

11. $16 \div 4 = \boxed{}$

12. $8 \div 4 = \boxed{}$

13. $9\overline{)27}$ with quotient 3

$\mathbf{9 \times 3 = 27}$

14. $9\overline{)36}$

15. $9\overline{)81}$

16. $6\overline{)54}$

17. $9\overline{)63}$

18. $5\overline{)45}$

19. $7\overline{)56}$

20. $7\overline{)49}$

21. $8\overline{)64}$

22. $5\overline{)25}$

23. $3\overline{)9}$

24. $6\overline{)18}$

Relating Multiplication and Division

Solve to find the missing number. Write a related multiplication fact under each problem.

1. _____ $\div 2 = 7$

2. $21 \div$ _____ $= 7$

3. _____ $\div 6 = 3$

4. $6 \div 2 =$ _____

5. $9 \div$ _____ $= 3$

6. _____ $\div 2 = 9$

7. $16 \div$ _____ $= 4$

8. _____ $\div 8 = 3$

9. _____ $\div 3 = 5$

10. $20 \div 5 =$ _____

11. $10 \div$ _____ $= 5$

12. _____ $\div 7 = 8$

13. $2 \div 1 =$ _____

14. $64 \div$ _____ $= 8$

15. _____ $\div 4 = 9$

Relating Multiplication and Division   ▲ Fact Families

Solve to find the missing number. Then, write the other problems in the fact family.

1. _____ ÷ 3 = 9

_____

_____

_____

2. 21 ÷ 7 = _____

_____

_____

_____

3. 48 ÷ _____ = 6

_____

_____

_____

4. 6 × _____ = 36

_____

5. 8 × 9 = _____

_____

_____

_____

6. _____ × 9 = 36

_____

_____

_____

7. 20 ÷ _____ = 5

_____

_____

_____

8. _____ ÷ 5 = 8

_____

_____

_____

9. 54 ÷ 9 = _____

_____

_____

_____

10. _____ × 4 = 28

_____

_____

_____

11. 6 × 5 = _____

_____

_____

_____

12. 10 × _____ = 70

_____

_____

_____

13. 42 ÷ 7 = _____

_____

_____

14. _____ ÷ 8 = 8

_____

15. 81 ÷ _____ = 9

_____

Division Poke Cards

Directions: Choose a card, find the missing number, and then poke a pencil through the hole you think is the correct answer. To check, turn the card over to see if the pencil is inserted through the circled hole.

$63 \div \underline{\hspace{1cm}} = 7$ 9 6 5 ● ● ●	$\underline{\hspace{1cm}} \div 6 = 4$ 16 24 36 ● ● ●	$18 \div 3 = \underline{\hspace{1cm}}$ 8 9 6 ● ● ●
$30 \div \underline{\hspace{1cm}} = 3$ 6 9 10 ● ● ●	$\underline{\hspace{1cm}} \div 7 = 5$ 30 35 40 ● ● ●	$27 \div 3 = \underline{\hspace{1cm}}$ 5 9 2 ● ● ●
$36 \div \underline{\hspace{1cm}} = 6$ 9 5 6 ● ● ●	$\underline{\hspace{1cm}} \div 8 = 7$ 45 24 56 ● ● ●	$28 \div 4 = \underline{\hspace{1cm}}$ 9 6 7 ● ● ●
$40 \div \underline{\hspace{1cm}} = 8$ 5 8 4 ● ● ●	$\underline{\hspace{1cm}} \div 8 = 4$ 36 32 42 ● ● ●	$54 \div 9 = \underline{\hspace{1cm}}$ 7 3 6 ● ● ●
$12 \div \underline{\hspace{1cm}} = 4$ 2 5 3 ● ● ●	$\underline{\hspace{1cm}} \div 1 = 9$ 8 10 9 ● ● ●	$48 \div 8 = \underline{\hspace{1cm}}$ 6 10 2 ● ● ●

To prep: If desired, print on card stock. Cut out the cards and laminate them for durability. Use a hole punch to punch holes over the black circles on each card. Then, use a permanent marker to circle the correct hole on the back of the card.

Finding Unknown Numbers

 ## Essential Question

How can you find a missing number in a multiplication or division problem?

Warm-Up/Review

Have students share the inverse operation of various division and multiplication problems. For example, "What is the inverse equation of 3 × 4 = 12?" (12 ÷ 4 = 3) "What is the inverse equation of 56 ÷ 7 = 8?" (8 × 7 = 56)

 ## Mini-Lesson

1. Write *10 ÷ 2 = 5* on the board. Write *dividend* under the 10, write *divisor* under the 2, and write *quotient* under the 5.

2. Explain that in order to find the missing divisor in a division problem, you divide the dividend by the quotient to find your answer. (10 ÷ 5 = 2) To find the missing dividend in a division problem, you multiply the divisor by the quotient to find your answer. (2 × 5 = 10) Remind students about using known facts to find unknown numbers. (For example, *what times 3 equals 27?*)

3. Write *14 ÷ ? = 7*. Say, "When you divide 14, the dividend, by 7, the quotient, you get 2. Therefore, 14 ÷ 2 = 7." Next, write *? ÷ 5 = 4*. Say, "When you multiply 5, the divisor, by 4, the quotient, you get 20. Therefore, 20 ÷ 5 = 4."

4. Write *3 × 5 = 15* on the board. Write *factor* under both 3 and 5, and write *product* under the 15. Explain that to find an unknown factor in a multiplication problem, you divide the product by the known factor. (15 ÷ 5 = 3 or 15 ÷ 3 = 5)

5. Write *8 × ? = 32*. Say, "When you divide 32, the product, by 8, the known factor, you get 4. Therefore, 8 × 4 = 32."

6. Have students continue practicing with other multiplication and division problems with unknown numbers.

 ## Math Talk

Why is knowing about inverse operations helpful when finding unknown numbers?
What is a real-world situation in which you would need to find an unknown number?
Is there another strategy to find unknown numbers? If so, explain.

 ## Journal Prompt

Write a multiplication or division problem with a missing number. Explain in your own words how to find the unknown number.

Materials

counters
sticky notes

 Workstations

Activity sheets (pages 35–37)
Unknown Number Poke Cards
(page 38)
Division Poke Cards (page 32)
Multiplication and division facts
flash cards

 Guided Math

○ **Remediation: Working with Counters**

1. Place counters within students' reach. Write $4 \times$ _____ $= 16$.

2. Point to the 16. Say, "This number is the product and tells us how many to start with." Ask students to take 16 counters.

3. Point to the 4. Say, "This number is the known factor and tells us how many groups to make." Have students draw 4 large circles. Demonstrate how to place the counters one at a time, dividing them evenly between the 4 groups. Explain, "The answer, or the unknown number, is how many counters are in each group. What is the unknown number?" Read the complete problem together: "4 times 4 equals 16."

4. Write $18 \div$ _____ $= 6$. Repeat steps 1–3 to find the missing divisor.

5. Have students continue practicing with similar problems.

☐ **On Level: Determining Missing Numbers**

1. Write the number 24. Ask students to write a multiplication equation that equals 24 on each side of the equal sign. Record their answers. Some possibilities include $2 \times 12 = 6 \times 4$ and $3 \times 8 = 1 \times 24$.

2. Now, choose one of the problems and cover one of its numbers with a sticky note. Ask, "How can we calculate the missing number? Is there only one possibility for the number? What if a number were missing from each side of the equation?"

3. Write the number 3. Ask students to write a division equation that equals 3 on each side of the equal sign. Record their answers. Some possibilities include $15 \div 5 = 18 \div 6$, $6 \div 2 = 9 \div 3$, $12 \div 4 = 21 \div 7$, and $24 \div 8 = 27 \div 9$. Repeat step 2, asking the same questions.

4. Have students write their own balanced equations. Give each student a sticky note to cover one number in her equation. Have groups work together to solve for each unknown number. Uncover the notes to check the answers.

△ **Enrichment: Solving for Variables**

1. Write the number sentence $8 \times n = 56$. Ask, "What does the n stand for?"

2. Discuss various strategies to solve the problem. Ask, "What are some mental math strategies that can help solve this problem? What operation can be performed on the known numbers to find the value of the variable?"

3. Write five problems: $4 \times n = 32$; $n \times 8 = 64$; $2 \times n = 16$; $n \times 6 = 36$; $7 \times n = 63$. Have students solve for n in each equation.

4. Write the number sentence $72 \div n = 8$. Repeat steps 2 and 3 with division problems.

5. Ask students to describe how they solved the problems. Encourage students to verbalize their solutions. Ask, "What do you know about numbers that helped you solve each equation?"

 Assess and Extend

Have students solve the following problem: *Fiona wants to buy 6 pieces of bubble gum. Each piece costs the same amount. If Fiona spends 30¢ on 6 pieces, how much did each piece cost?* Students should write the multiplication sentence and the division sentence used to solve the problem.

Name _____   Date _____

Finding Unknown Numbers   ● Working with Counters

Solve. Draw a picture to show how you solved each problem.

1. _____ × 4 = 12	**2.** 24 = _____ × 4
3. 15 ÷ _____ = 3	**4.** 7 = 14 ÷ _____
5. _____ × 5 = 45	**6.** 8 = _____ × 4
7. 6 × _____ = 12	**8.** 20 = 10 × _____
9. 30 ÷ _____ = 10	**10.** 6 = 24 ÷ _____
11. _____ ÷ 6 = 3	**12.** 8 = _____ ÷ 4

Finding Unknown Numbers   ☐ Determining Missing Numbers

Find the number that makes both number sentences true.

1. $3 \times$ _____ $= 12$

$16 \div$ _____ $= 4$

2. $16 = 4 \times$ _____

$8 \div$ _____ $= 2$

3. _____ $\times 3 = 15$

_____ $\div 1 = 5$

4. $12 =$ _____ $\times 6$

$18 \div$ _____ $= 9$

5. $6 \times 4 =$ _____

_____ $\div 3 = 8$

6. _____ $= 4 \times 9$

$6 \times 6 =$ _____

7. $6 \times$ _____ $= 18$

$3 \times$ _____ $= 9$

8. $35 = 7 \times$ _____

$45 \div$ _____ $= 9$

9. _____ $\times 4 = 32$

$16 \div$ _____ $= 2$

10. $30 =$ _____ $\times 5$

$42 \div 7 =$ _____

11. $16 \div$ _____ $= 2$

_____ $\times 7 = 56$

12. $1 = 8 \div$ _____

$64 \div$ _____ $= 8$

13. $25 \div 5 =$ _____

$40 \div$ _____ $= 8$

14. _____ $= 63 \div 7$

$27 \div 3 =$ _____

15. _____ $\div 4 = 3$

$6 \times 2 =$ _____

16. $49 =$ _____ $\times 7$

_____ $= 56 \div 8$

17. $28 \div$ _____ $= 7$

_____ $\times 5 = 20$

18. $4 = 36 \div$ _____

$3 \times 3 =$ _____

19. _____ $\div 2 = 3$

$54 \div$ _____ $= 9$

20. $5 =$ _____ $\div 3$

_____ $= 30 \div 2$

21. _____ $\times 3 = 21$

$28 \div$ _____ $= 4$

Finding Unknown Numbers   ▲ Solving for Variables

Write the number that makes the equation true. Then, write the multiplication or division problem that helped you solve the problem.

1. $1 \times n = 7$ $n =$ _____ _____	**2.** $n \times 3 = 18$ $n =$ _____ _____	**3.** $5 \times 4 = n$ $n =$ _____ _____
4. $n \div 16 = 2$ $n =$ _____ _____	**5.** $16 \div n = 8$ $n =$ _____ _____	**6.** $63 \div n = 7$ $n =$ _____ _____
7. $18 = 2 \times n$ $n =$ _____ _____	**8.** $24 \div 2 = n$ $n =$ _____ _____	**9.** $4 \times 6 = 3 \times n$ $n =$ _____ _____
10. $n \div 9 = 4$ $n =$ _____ _____	**11.** $5 \times n = 3 \times 10$ $n =$ _____ _____	**12.** $48 = n \times 8$ $n =$ _____ _____

Unknown Number Poke Cards

Directions: Choose a card, find the missing number, and then poke a pencil through the hole you think is the correct answer. To check, turn the card over to see if the pencil is inserted through the circled hole.

$54 \div \rule{1cm}{0.4pt} = 6$	$5 \times \rule{1cm}{0.4pt} = 40$
9 6 5 ● ● ●	8 10 4 ● ● ●
$\rule{1cm}{0.4pt} \div 3 = 5$	$\rule{1cm}{0.4pt} \times 7 = 49$
13 15 17 ● ● ●	5 6 7 ● ● ●
$30 \div 5 = \rule{1cm}{0.4pt}$	$9 \times 3 = \rule{1cm}{0.4pt}$
8 6 9 ● ● ●	17 27 37 ● ● ●
$49 \div \rule{1cm}{0.4pt} = 7$	$6 \times \rule{1cm}{0.4pt} = 12$
4 8 7 ● ● ●	3 4 2 ● ● ●
$\rule{1cm}{0.4pt} \div 8 = 9$	$\rule{1cm}{0.4pt} \times 6 = 24$
48 72 62 ● ● ●	3 4 5 ● ● ●
$42 \div 6 = \rule{1cm}{0.4pt}$	$2 \times \rule{1cm}{0.4pt} = 14$
4 7 9 ● ● ●	9 7 4 ● ● ●
$18 \div \rule{1cm}{0.4pt} = 3$	$\rule{1cm}{0.4pt} \times 5 = 20$
5 8 6 ● ● ●	4 1 10 ● ● ●
$\rule{1cm}{0.4pt} \div 4 = 9$	$6 \times 6 = \rule{1cm}{0.4pt}$
36 26 42 ● ● ●	26 16 36 ● ● ●

To prep: If desired, print on card stock. Cut out the cards and laminate them for durability. Use a hole punch to punch holes over the black circles on each card. Then, use a permanent marker to circle the correct hole on the back of the card.

Two-Step Word Problems

 Essential Question

How can two-step word problems be solved using the four operations and a letter for the unknown?

 Warm-Up/Review

Show the following problem: *Ben wants to plant pumpkins. He bought 6 seed packets. Each packet contains 5 seeds. How many seeds does Ben have to plant?* Have students solve, then share their answer and strategy with a partner.

 Mini-Lesson

Materials: copies of word problems (see below)

1. Give each student a copy of the following problem: *Aaron and his scout troop hiked 3 miles and then rested. After their break, they hiked another 3 miles. The total distance of the hike was 8 miles. How many more miles did they need to go before reaching their destination?*

2. Explain, "First we need to add the total distance hiked so far." Model adding 3 + 3 to find 6 miles.

3. "Then, we need to subtract this sum from the total to find the remaining distance." Model the subtraction to find 2 miles. "So, the scouts must hike another 2 miles to reach their destination."

4. Remind students that when solving a multi-step word problem, you must break the problem down into individual steps and solve one at a time.

5. Give students another problem to solve with a partner: *Brad had 74 baseball cards. He decided to keep 11 and share the rest with his 9 friends. How many baseball cards did each of his friends receive?* (7) Have students explain how they broke the problem down into individual steps and solved each step.

 Math Talk

How could you make it easier to recognize the individual steps in a word problem?
Name another strategy you could use to solve this problem.
What is the most challenging thing about solving word problems?

 Journal Prompt

Explain in your own words how to solve a two-step word problem.

Materials

copies of word problems (see below)
highlighters

 Workstations

Activity sheets (pages 41–43)
Multi-Step Word Problem Task
Cards (page 44)

 Guided Math

○ **Remediation: Drawing Pictures to Solve Word Problems**

1. Display the following problem: *Our family drove 345 miles on vacation. We crossed 3 states. We stopped 3 times in 2 states, and 2 times in the last state. How many times did we stop?*

2. Explain, "First, we need to determine the question. It asks, 'How many times did we stop?' So, the first statement about stops says, 'We stopped 3 times in 2 states.'" Draw 2 circles for states, and draw 3 dots in each circle to represent how many times the family stopped in each state. Explain, "Three times 2 is 6 stops."

3. Say, "Then, it says, 'We stopped 2 times in the last state.'" Draw 1 circle for the state and draw 2 dots in the circle to represent the stops. "Two times 1 is 2 stops. Six stops plus 2 stops is 8 stops. So, the family stopped 8 times altogether."

4. Explain, "Sometimes there is extra information in word problems. For example, the number of miles in this problem does not give us any useful information."

5. Continue with visual, concrete examples. Encourage students to draw or act out each problem.

☐ **On Level: Clues for Solving Word Problems**

1. Display the following problem: *We went to an amusement park. There were 5 roller coasters. Jan rode each one 4 times. Hunter rode each one 3 times. How many times did Jan and Hunter ride them in all?* (35) Have students solve the problem on their own and list key words from the problem.

2. Explain that students can search for clues to help write an equation. First, students should determine what the problem is asking (how many times they rode roller coasters in all). In this problem, the question uses the words *in all*, which signals addition. The problem also says each person rode each roller coaster a certain amount of times, which indicates multiplication. Model how to identify and highlight the numbers and key words in the problem. Work together to create a list of key words for each operation.

3. Use the key words to determine the number sentence needed to solve the problem. Ask, "Which operations did you use? What numbers did you combine?"

4. Practice identifying key words in other word problems and writing the corresponding equations.

△ **Enrichment: Writing Word Problems**

1. Write $(4 \times 12) + (3 \times 12) = 84$. Remind students that parentheses tell them what to do first in a problem.

2. Ask students to write a word problem to describe the equation. Say, "Multiplication deals with sets or groups of things. What things come in sets of 12? What word signals addition?" Write the example, "Kyle was baking cupcakes for the bake sale. He went to the store and bought 4 dozen eggs. When we got home, he realized he needed more. So, he went back and bought 3 dozen more. How many eggs did Kyle buy in all?" Ask, "Which part of the story says to write 4×12? 3×12? What words suggest using parentheses? Which part says to add the two amounts together?"

3. Direct students to write their own word problems for the same equation. Discuss students' stories. Have students identify and highlight the key words in their stories.

 Assess and Extend

Have students solve the following problem: *In Mrs. Wu's class, 9 girls and 6 boys each have an eraser collection. Each girl has 7 erasers in her collection, and each boy has 5 erasers in his collection. How many erasers do the boys and girls have altogether?* (93)

Two-Step Word Problems

Read each problem. Solve. Draw a picture or write equations to show your work for both parts of the problem.

1. Bonnie bought 8 boxes of chocolate chip cookies and 6 boxes of peanut butter cookies. Each chocolate chip cookie box has 9 cookies and each peanut butter cookie box has 8 cookies. How many cookies does Bonnie have in all?

2. Michelle slices 6 apples into 6 slices each. She then shares the apples with 3 of her friends. If Michelle and each of her friends get the same number of apple slices, how many will they each get?

3. We hiked 8 miles on both Saturday and Sunday. We rode our bikes 15 miles on Monday and 16 miles on Tuesday. How far did we travel altogether?

4. Malia reads books in the car. On one trip, she read 87 pages. On another trip, she read 108 pages. If the book is 232 pages long, how many pages does she have left to read?

5. Jack's goal is to find 500 insects. In one park, he counted 222 bugs. In another park, he counted 187 bugs. How many more insects does he need to find?

6. Lucy found 14 flowers in her backyard. She found 11 more in her neighbor's yard. She divided the flowers equally between 5 vases. How many flowers did she put in each vase?

Name _____   Date _____

Two-Step Word Problems   ☐ Clues for Solving Word Problems

Identify the key words in each problem by circling them. Identify the key numbers by drawing a triangle around them. Then, solve each problem.

1. Lisa and Melissa have each blown up 6 balloons. They need a total of 20 balloons for the party at school. How many more balloons do they need to blow up?

2. Luke has collected a total of 34 cans and boxes of food for the food drive. Cole has collected 29. Their team goal was to collect 95 cans and boxes of food altogether. How many more do they need to collect to reach their goal?

3. Yesterday, Evan picked 43 apples. Today, he picked another 65 apples. His father asked him to divide the total in half so they could share their apples with the food bank. How many apples did they donate?

4. Reese, Tracy, and Ruby each raised $5 for the fund-raiser at school by selling pretzels at the carnival. They need a total of $25 to reach their goal. How much more do they need to raise to reach their goal?

5. Simon pays $8 each time he goes to the water park to swim. He has already been there 5 times this summer! How many more times can he go before he spends a total of $104?

6. Yolanda loves to draw. She draws on 9 sheets of her pad a day. She's had her 105-page drawing pad for 9 days. How many clean pages does she have left?

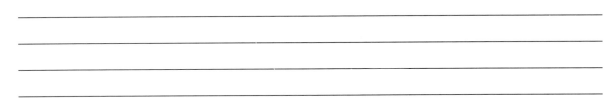

Two-Step Word Problems   ▲ Writing Word Problems

Write a word problem to describe each equation.

1. (3 × 9) – 10

_____

_____

_____

_____

2. (4 × 8) – 5

_____

_____

_____

_____

3. (3 × 9) + (4 × 7)

_____

_____

_____

_____

4. 6 × (2 + 2)

_____

_____

_____

_____

5. (7 × 9) + (21 ÷ 7)

_____

_____

_____

_____

Multi-Step Word Problem Task Cards

There are 3 kinds of stamps available at the post office. They cost 5¢, 27¢, or 42¢. Timothy buys three 5¢ stamps and four 27¢ stamps. How much money did Timothy spend on stamps?

A

Daniel makes fruit baskets to give to his family. Daniel puts 3 pears, 5 bananas, and 6 apples in each basket. How many pieces of fruit will he need to make 3 fruit baskets?

B

Emily and Ivan each make a photo album. Emily can fit 3 photos on each page of her album. She fills 9 pages. Ivan can fit 4 photos on each page of his album. He fills 7 pages. Who has the most photos in their album, Emily or Ivan?

C

Kenneth is buying school supplies. Pencils come in packages of 4 and erasers come in boxes of 9. If Kenneth buys 4 packages of pencils and 8 boxes of erasers, how many total pencils and erasers will he have bought?

D

Jeffrey is opening a pet store. He has 12 turtles, 15 snails, and 25 goldfish that he will put into fish tanks around the store. Jeffrey has 3 tanks for turtles and snails. How many turtles and snails are going to be in each tank altogether?

E

Lola volunteers at the hospital. She volunteered 33 hours in May and 41 hours in June. She volunteered 4 more hours in July than she did in June. How many total hours did Lola volunteer in the last 3 months?

F

Mrs. Hamilton bakes 63 cupcakes. She saves 3 cupcakes for her grandchildren and gives the rest away to 10 of her neighbors. If she gives each neighbor the same number of cupcakes, how many cupcakes did each of Mrs. Hamilton's neighbors get?

G

A third-grade teacher bought 11 boxes of crayons. Of the boxes, 6 had 9 crayons, and the other 5 boxes had 10 crayons. How many crayons did the third-grade teacher buy in all?

H

To prep: If desired, copy the task cards on card stock for durability. Cut them apart and place in a center. Write the answer on the back of each card to make them self-checking.

Arithmetic Patterns

 Essential Question

How can the properties of operations help to identify and explain numeric patterns?

 Warm-Up/Review

Show students a pattern of shapes, such as *circle, square, triangle, heart; circle, square, triangle, heart*. Have students identify the pattern that they see.

 Mini-Lesson

1. Write the numbers *1, 3, 5,* and *7* on the board. Ask "What number comes next? How do you know?" Draw the numbers in a line on the board. Draw "hops" in between adjacent numbers and label each "hop" with *+2* to show the pattern.

2. Explain, "The next number is 9 because each time you are skipping one number, which is the same as adding 2 to the previous number. Also, all of the numbers in this pattern are odd."

3. Write the numbers *1, 4, 7,* and *10* on the board. Ask for the next two numbers. (13, 16) When students share their answers, ask them to identify the pattern and explain how they figure it out. (+3)

4. Write the numbers *6, 10, 8, 12,* and *10* on the board. Ask students to find the next two numbers (14, 12). Explain that this number pattern has 2 steps. The first is +4. The second step is –2. If needed, draw and label the "hops" to make the pattern clearer.

5. Continue practicing with different numbers and different patterns. Students should be able to explain the patterns. They should try and apply them to each number they are given to be sure it works each time.

 Math Talk

Can number patterns have more than one rule? Explain.

What does it mean when the pattern has two steps?

Show a way to organize a number pattern.

 Journal Prompt

Write the next 3 numbers in this number pattern: *1, 1, 2, 3, 5, 8.* (13, 21, 34) Explain what the rule is in words. (Add the previous two numbers.)

Materials

(none)

 Workstations

Activity sheets (pages 47–49)
Number Pattern Puzzles (page 50)

 Guided Math

⊙ **Remediation: Introducing Charts**

1. Draw a picture of 3 cows. Ask, "If each cow has 4 legs, how many legs are in this picture?"
2. Ask, "What if 1 more cow arrives? How many legs would there be? What if there were 10 cows?" Discuss strategies for calculating the answer. Students might draw pictures, continue counting, or use repeated addition or multiplication.
3. Draw a T-chart that shows the number of cows in the first column and the number of legs in the second column. Ask, "What operation is done to the number of cows to find how many legs there are altogether? To solve for 5 cows, I can multiply 5 times 4. Or, I can continue my pattern, counting by 4s (4, 8, 12, 16, 20). Do these strategies still work with 10 cows? Twenty cows?"
4. Continue with other examples. Encourage using concrete visual strategies.

▢ **On Level: Working with Number Patterns**

1. Show students a T-chart with *1, 2, 3* and *4* in the left column and *3, 6, 9,* and *12* in the right column. Ask what this chart could represent. Accept all reasonable answers. Suggest that these are wheels on a tricycle. "One tricycle has 3 wheels, 2 tricycles have 6 wheels, etc. Are the numbers on the right side greater or less than the numbers on the left side? What operations are used to make numbers larger? What is an addition rule for this chart? What is a multiplication rule for this chart?" (Each time, 3 is added to the number in the wheel column, or the number of tricycles is multiplied by 3.)
2. Ask students to continue this chart through 10 tricycles. Discuss how they found the answers.
3. Now, ask students to create charts of their own. Observe to see if students stay consistent with a rule and apply it to each number.
4. Have the group calculate the rules on each other's charts.

△ **Enrichment: Input/Output Charts**

1. Draw an input/output chart with inputs *20, 15, 10,* and *5* and outputs *4, 3, 2,* and *1*. Ask, "Are the numbers on the right greater or less than the numbers on the left? What operation can be applied to the numbers in the left column to get the numbers in the right column?"
2. Draw another input/output chart with four input numbers. Leave out two numbers on the input side, but provide the corresponding output numbers. Ask, "What is the rule for this input/output chart? How can you find the missing input numbers?"
3. Ask students to create their own input/output charts with at least five input numbers. Have them leave a few numbers off the chart to make it more difficult for the group to solve. Also, challenge students to write charts with two-step rules, such as *×3, +2*.
4. Have students share their charts and have other students calculate the rules.

 Assess and Extend

Have students solve the following problem: *The community swimming pool uses chemical drops every day to keep the pool clean. The chemical is added in a pattern to keep up with the number of people swimming. On Sunday, 1 drop is added; on Monday, 2 drops are added; on Tuesday, 4 drops are added; and on Wednesday, 8 drops are added. How many drops will be added on Thursday?* (16) *Friday?* (32) Students should explain the rule to the pattern in words. (×2)

Arithmetic Patterns

⬤ Introducing Charts

Write the rule for each chart.

1. Rule: _____

Input	Output
4	14
8	18
10	20
55	65

2. Rule: _____

Input	Output
100	95
45	40
30	25
15	10

3. Rule: _____

Input	Output
3	12
8	17
11	20
20	29

4. Rule: _____

Input	Output
4	11
12	19
22	29
38	45

5. Rule: _____

Input	Output
15	12
24	21
32	29
54	51

6. Rule: _____

Input	Output
8	16
5	10
11	22
10	20

Arithmetic Patterns   ☐ Working with Number Patterns

Write the rule for each chart. Then, fill in the missing numbers. For problems 7 and 8, create your own input/output charts.

1. Rule: _____

Input	Output
100	90
60	50
30	20
20	10

2. Rule: _____

Input	Output
125	140
170	___
305	320
380	___

3. Rule: _____

Input	Output
3	18
5	30
8	___
11	___

4. Rule: _____

Input	Output
245	___
550	575
810	835
925	___

5. Rule: _____

Input	Output
5	25
6	___
8	___
9	81

6. Rule: _____

Input	Output
45	195
150	300
240	___
300	___

7. Rule: _____

Input	Output

8. Rule: _____

Input	Output

Arithmetic Patterns   ▲ Input/Output Charts

Write the rule for each chart. Then, fill in the missing numbers. For problems 7 and 8, create your own input/output charts.

1. Rule: _____

Input	Output
800	650
___	500
500	___
350	200

2. Rule: _____

Input	Output
34	68
42	84
68	___
___	160

3. Rule: _____

Input	Output
25	75
75	___
85	255
___	315

4. Rule: _____

Input	Output
40	402
50	502
60	602
70	___

5. Rule: _____

Input	Output
3	16
5	26
6	___
8	___

6. Rule: _____

Input	Output
700	350
___	250
300	150
___	50

7. Rule: _____

Input	Output

8. Rule: _____

Input	Output

Number Pattern Puzzles

Directions: Assemble the three puzzles. The piece with the star is the first piece to each puzzle. Use the pattern in the numbers at the bottom of the puzzle pieces to help you find and place the pieces correctly.

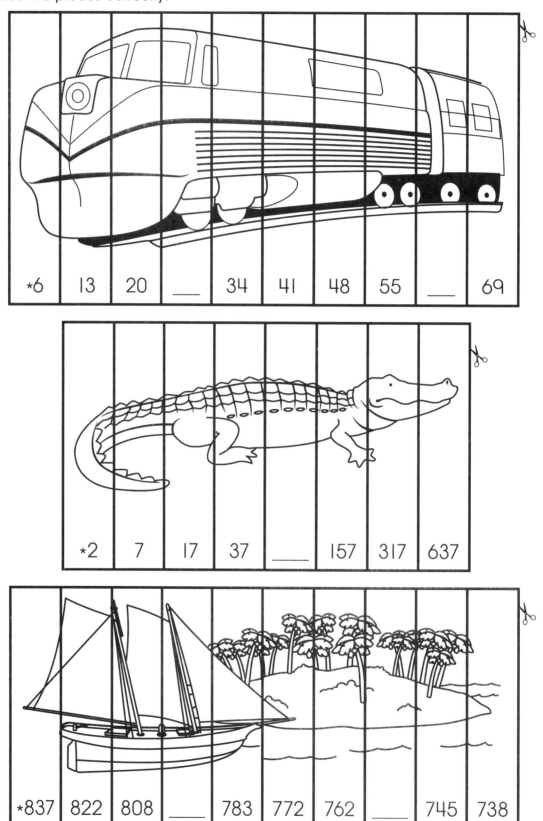

| *6 | 13 | 20 | ___ | 34 | 41 | 48 | 55 | ___ | 69 |

| *2 | 7 | 17 | 37 | ___ | 157 | 317 | 637 |

| *837 | 822 | 808 | ___ | 783 | 772 | 762 | ___ | 745 | 738 |

To prep: If desired, print on card stock nund laminate for durability. Cut on the solid lines to separate the pieces. Place in a center with the directions. Copy on several colors of card stock to make several sets.

Reading and Writing Numbers

 Essential Question

How do I read and write numbers to 100,000?

Warm-Up/Review

Write the number 542 on the board. Review place value by asking students, "What number is in the ones place? Tens place? Hundreds place?"

 Mini-Lesson

Materials: index cards, tape, sticky notes, number cards 0–9, base ten blocks

1. Write *ones*, *tens*, *hundreds*, *thousands*, *ten thousands*, and *hundred thousands* on index cards. Tape the cards onto the board in order. Explain that the place value names help us talk about the digits and know their values.

2. Write *128,567* under the index cards. Ask, "What is the place value of the digit 8? What is its value? Is it worth only 8?" Explain, "It means that there are 8 thousands. Its value is 8,000." Demonstrate skip counting by 1,000 8 times until you get to 8,000.

3. Now, use sticky notes to cover everything except the digits 6 and 7. Ask, "What if I used an addition problem to show the values in 67? What would the problem look like?" Lead students to use the value of each digit in its place to write the addends. Write *60 + 7*. Extend to the hundreds place. "The value of 5 hundreds is 500." Add this to the above addition sentence and explain that writing the number in this way is called *expanded form*. Continue removing sticky notes and writing the value of each digit to complete the expanded form.

4. Continue working with other numbers, focusing on the place value names, their values, and using expanded form.

 Math Talk

How much larger is this digit than that one? How do you know?
Can you explain how this is related to expanded form?
What is the purpose of the 0?

 Journal Prompt

Create and record a 6-digit number. Write the number in word form and tell how much each digit is worth.

Materials

index cards with place value
names (see below)
0–9 number cards
base ten blocks

 Workstations

Activity sheets (pages 53–55)
Place Value Tic-Tac-Toe (page 56)

 Guided Math

○ **Remediation: Using Manipulatives**

1. Give each student index cards with place value names written on them (*ones, tens, hundreds, thousands*). Also, make number cards and base ten blocks available.
2. Have students put the index cards in the correct order in front of them. Using number cards, have them show you *2,345*. Now, have them place the correct number of base ten blocks under each digit. Ask, "What digit is in the hundreds place? Which place is the 2 in?"
3. To determine the value of each number, count base ten blocks with the group. Ask, "How much does the 4 stand for? How much does the 5 stand for?"
4. Have students help you write the number in expanded form. Explain as you go, "There are 2 thousands, so the value is 2,000. There are 3 hundreds, so the value is 300. Four tens is 40, and 5 ones is 5."

▢ **On Level: Expanded Form**

1. Give each student a set of number cards, as well as index cards with the place value names written on them (*ones, tens, hundreds, thousands, ten thousands, hundred thousands*).
2. Have students show you the number *321,809* by arranging the number cards under the place value cards.
3. Ask, "What digit is in the thousands place? What is the value of the 3? What is the place name of the 9?" Have students replace all of the number cards after the named digit with 0s to see its value.
4. Now, write *400 + 30,000 + 5*. Ask students to write the number in standard form. Ask, "What did you do when you noticed the numbers were not in descending order? How did you handle the missing tens place value?"
5. Continue working with other numbers. Eventually, remove the index cards and have students work without them.

△ **Enrichment: Numbers to the Millions**

1. Give students a set of number cards and have them each choose six cards at random.
2. Have students make the smallest and then the largest number possible with the digits. Ask, "How did you make your decision to place the digits? How did you handle zeros?"
3. Write *329,513*. Have students write the number in expanded form. Ask, "If I added 6 ten thousands to this number, what would be the sum? (335,513) What if I added 10 hundreds? (330,513)" Have students use mental math and their knowledge of place value to solve the problems.
4. Write *63*. Ask, "What happens if I multiply 10 times 63? What about 100 times 63 or 1,000 times 63?" Discuss how knowing place value is helpful for solving problems.
5. Continue adding, subtracting, and multiplying with other numbers using place value as a guide.

 Assess and Extend

Have students describe the difference between each 3 in the number 333,333.

Name _____   Date _____

Reading and Writing Numbers   ● Using Manipulatives

Write the place and the value of each underlined digit.

Number	Place	Value
3<u>4</u>5	_____ tens _____	_____ 40 _____
1. 2,1<u>3</u>4	_____	_____
2. 8<u>7</u>	_____	_____
3. <u>7</u>63	_____	_____
4. <u>6</u>,004	_____	_____
5. 9,<u>5</u>33	_____	_____
6. <u>4</u>87	_____	_____
7. 8,<u>2</u>09	_____	_____
8. 7<u>4</u>7	_____	_____
9. 9<u>1</u>	_____	_____
10. <u>8</u>,235	_____	_____

Write the expanded form of each number.

11. 971 _____

12. 2,145 _____

13. 86 _____

14. 6,230 _____

15. 952 _____

Write the standard form of each expanded number.

16. 700 + 40 + 3 _____

17. 500 + 10 + 2 _____

18. 70 + 6 _____

19. 1,000 + 400 + 30 _____

20. 3,000 + 600 + 30 + 7 _____

Reading and Writing Numbers   ▢ Expanded Form

Write the place and the value of each underlined digit.

Number	Place	Value
1. <u>5</u>,879	_____	_____
2. 8,<u>1</u>23	_____	_____
3. 7,00<u>4</u>	_____	_____
4. <u>3</u>21,467	_____	_____
5. 4,<u>2</u>34	_____	_____
6. 6,9<u>8</u>7	_____	_____
7. 8<u>9</u>3,072	_____	_____
8. 5,02<u>8</u>	_____	_____
9. <u>2</u>,369	_____	_____
10. 4,0<u>0</u>9	_____	_____

Write the expanded form of each number.

11. 5,897 _____

12. 2,308 _____

13. 76,450 _____

14. 7,876 _____

15. 224,341 _____

Write the standard form of each expanded number.

16. 400,000 + 20,000 + 1,000 + 300 + 60 + 1 _____

17. 4,000 + 600 + 80 + 1 _____

18. 3,000 + 500 + 20 + 3 _____

19. 10 + 5,000 + 600,000 + 500 + 80,000 _____

20. 700 + 30 + 4,000 + 5 _____

Reading and Writing Numbers ▲ Numbers to the Millions

Write the place and the value of each underlined digit.

Number	Place	Value
1. 28,9<u>0</u>8	_____	_____
2. 57,<u>1</u>45	_____	_____
3. 32,82<u>4</u>	_____	_____
4. <u>9</u>,008	_____	_____
5. <u>9</u>8,876	_____	_____

Write the expanded form of each number.

6. 38,812 _____

7. 678,933 _____

8. 59,004 _____

9. 40,045 _____

10. 9,733,312 _____

Write the standard form of each expanded number.

11. 30,000 + 4,000 + 700 + 50 + 3 _____

12. 60,000 + 3,000 + 400 + 70 + 1 _____

13. 4,000 + 1 + 2,000,000 + 700,000 + 500 + 30,000 _____

14. 50,000 + 20 + 7 _____

15. 7,000 + 4 + 70 + 200 + 60,000 _____

Solve each equation.

16. 45,345 + 10,000 _____

17. 67,432 + 30,000 _____

18. 94 × 10 _____

19. 67 × 1,000 _____

20. 854 × 100 _____

Place Value Tic-Tac-Toe

Materials: dry-erase markers or two-color counters, several sets of 0–9 number cards, scrap paper

To play: Shuffle the number cards and place them facedown in a draw pile. Players take turns. Use the number cards to solve the problem on a space. Use scrap paper as needed. If the player solves a problem correctly, she uses a counter to cover the space or marks an *X* or *O* with a dry-erase marker. The first player to get three spaces in a row wins.

Choose 6 cards. Make the smallest 6-digit number you can with the cards. Read it aloud.	Choose 3 cards. Make the largest 3-digit number you can. Write the number in word form.	Choose 4 cards. Make a 4-digit number. Write the number in word form.
Choose 5 cards. Make a 5-digit number. Write the number in expanded form.	Choose 5 cards. Make a 5-digit number. Tell the value of the number in the thousands place.	Choose 5 cards. Make a 5-digit number. Write the number in word form.
Choose 4 cards. Make a 4-digit number. Write the number in expanded form.	Choose 3 cards. Make a 3-digit number. Multiply it by 10 and write your answer in standard form.	Choose 6 cards. Make a 6-digit number. Write the number in word form.

To prep: Laminate the game board so it can be used with dry-erase markers. If needed, use index cards to create number cards with numbers 0–9. Cut off these directions before copying.

Rounding Numbers

Essential Question

How can numbers be rounded to the nearest 10 and nearest 100?

Warm-Up/Review

Write a 3-digit number on the board. Review the place of each digit and what the value of each digit is. Repeat with several more numbers, including those with 4 and 5 digits.

Mini-Lesson

Materials: sticky notes

1. Draw an illustration on the board of a hill with a car at the bottom left of the hill. Write the digits 1 to 9 along the hill so that 4 is slightly to the left of the top and 5 is slightly to the right of the top (see page 59 for an example). Explain, "This is a very large hill and a very weak car; it takes large numbers for the car to get over the hill."

2. Write 46 on a sticky note and place it on the car. Ask, "What 10 comes before 46? What is the next 10?" Write 40 and 50 on sticky notes and place them on either side of the hill.

3. Say, "This hill can help us figure out how to round 46 to the nearest 10. If the number in the ones place is 5 or greater, we round to the greater 10." Demonstrate how the car makes it to the 5 and rolls to the greater 10. "If the number in the ones column is 4 or less, we round down to the lesser 10." Change the number on the car to 44 and show the car going up to the 4 and rolling back down the hill.

4. Relate how using the hill illustration is like using a number line, and draw the number line showing the relationship.

5. Continue practicing with other numbers.

Math Talk

How does rounding make math easier?
Why do we round numbers?
When might you use rounding?

Journal Prompt

What is 99 rounded to the nearest 10? Explain how you rounded.

Materials

sticky notes
laminated blank number lines
dry-erase markers

 Workstations

Activity sheets (pages 59–61)
Rolling Round Up (or Down!)
(page 62)

 Guided Math

○ Remediation: Rounding to Tens and Hundreds

1. Ask students to draw the hill and the car. Have them label the hill with the digits 1 to 9.

2. Give each student a sticky note with *22* written on it. Have students place the notes on the drawn cars. "How do we figure out which two tens this number is between?" Point to the digit in the tens place and ask how this number gives a clue to the lesser 10. Then, have students find what 10 comes next by counting by tens. Have students write both tens on sticky notes and place them on either side of the hill.

3. Have students move their 22 notes to the number along the hill that matches the number in the ones place. Have students move their 22 notes back down the hill to the lesser 10. Ask students to explain when to round down to the lesser 10 and when to round up to the greater 10. Discuss how the number in the ones place lets us know whether to round up or down.

4. Repeat steps 2 and 3 with several more numbers less than 100. Then, move on to rounding to the hundreds place. Add zeros to the digits on the hill, and emphasize finding which two hundreds the number falls between.

☐ On Level: Rounding to Hundreds and Thousands

1. Give students number lines and dry-erase markers. Have them follow along on their own number lines as you model.

2. Write *257*. Ask, "How do we figure out which two hundreds this number is between?" Point to the digit in the hundreds place and ask how this number gives a clue to the lesser hundred. Then, ask students what hundred comes next. Write *200* and *300* on either side of the number line. Next, have students label the tens on the number line (210 through 290).

3. Ask students to explain when to round down to the lesser 100 and when to round up to the greater 100. Have them draw a slash through the number line to show the point that separates the tens that will round down and the tens that will round up. Discuss how the number in the tens place lets us know whether to round up or down.

4. Practice rounding with 3-digit and 4-digit numbers, using the number line as a guide.

△ Enrichment: Specific Place Value Rounding

1. Write *31,258*. Underline the 1 in the thousands place.

2. Explain that sometimes we need to round to a specific place value, not just the digit with the greatest place value.

3. Ask students to explain their strategies for rounding to the number in the thousands place if a number is in the ten thousands place. Say, "This number is between 31,000 and 32,000. Which one is it closer to? Which digit will help me figure out if I should round up or down? What happens to the numbers in the hundreds, tens, and ones places?"

4. Continue practicing with other large numbers, up to 6-digit numbers.

 Assess and Extend

Have students solve the following problem: *In an election for mayor, Ms. Beck received 83,913 votes, Mr. Daniels received 66,022 votes, Mrs. Gupta received 1,084 votes, and Mr. Kaya received 115,014 votes. Who won the election?* Round the winner's votes to the nearest ten thousand.

Rounding Numbers

● Rounding to Tens and Hundreds

Write the numbers 1 to 9 on the lines. Start at the car. Use the hill to help you solve the problems.

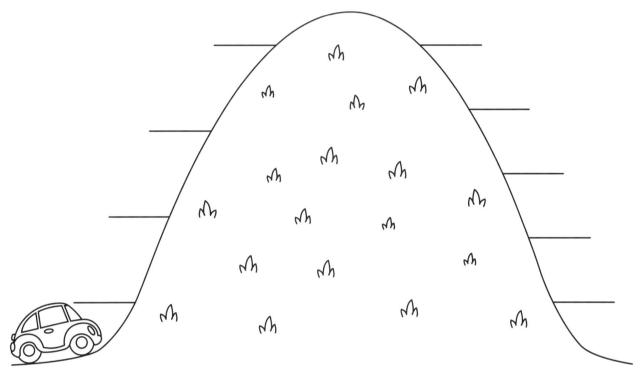

Round each number to the nearest ten.

1. 21 _____

2. 76 _____

3. 43 _____

4. 11 _____

5. 39 _____

6. 88 _____

7. 52 _____

8. 35 _____

9. 97 _____

10. 64 _____

Round each number to the nearest hundred.

11. 220 _____

12. 863 _____

13. 804 _____

14. 577 _____

15. 129 _____

16. 651 _____

17. 333 _____

18. 791 _____

19. 630 _____

20. 879 _____

Name _____   Date _____

 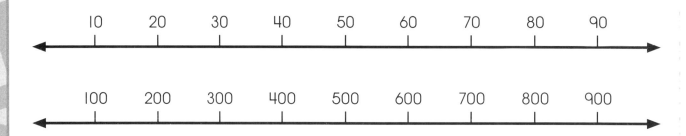

Use the number lines to help you round the numbers.

10   20   30   40   50   60   70   80   90

100   200   300   400   500   600   700   800   900

Round each number to the nearest hundred.

1. 235 _____

2. 756 _____

3. 891 _____

4. 211 _____

5. 172 _____

6. 649 _____

7. 372 _____

8. 501 _____

9. 391 _____

10. 428 _____

Round each number to the nearest thousand.

11. 1,872 _____

12. 9,124 _____

13. 4,871 _____

14. 6,199 _____

15. 8,293 _____

16. 2,009 _____

17. 5,877 _____

18. 3,500 _____

19. 7,220 _____

20. 9,701 _____

Rounding Numbers   ▲ Specific Place Value Rounding

Round each number to the underlined place value. Then, write the underlined digit's place value name.

	Rounded Number	**Place Value of Underlined Digit**
I. 2̲1	_____	_____
2. 14̲,874	_____	_____
3. 8̲,378	_____	_____
4. 3̲24	_____	_____
5. 6̲8,011	_____	_____
6. 73,98̲1	_____	_____
7. 8̲7	_____	_____
8. 4̲0,010	_____	_____
9. 5̲50	_____	_____
10. 4,6̲15	_____	_____
II. 6̲8	_____	_____
12. 4̲51	_____	_____
13. 10̲,009	_____	_____
14. 60̲2	_____	_____
15. 7̲,234	_____	_____
16. 81̲,513	_____	_____
17. 24̲1	_____	_____
18. 2,9̲92	_____	_____
19. 5̲2,876	_____	_____
20. 7̲16	_____	_____

Rolling Round Up
(or Down!)

Materials: 3 dice, two-color counters

To play: Players take turns. Roll 3 dice. Place the numbers in any order to create a 3-digit number. Then, round it to the nearest ten. Place your counter on the rounded number. If a counter is already on a space, you may not place your counter there. The first player with four counters in a row wins.

110	120	130	140	150	160	170
210	220	230	240	250	260	270
310	320	330	340	350	360	370
410	420	430	440	450	460	470
510	520	530	540	550	560	570
610	620	630	640	650	660	670

To prep: If desired, copy onto card stock and laminate for durability. Cut off these directions before copying.

Addition within 1,000

 Essential Question

How can strategies and step-by-step methods help with addition within 1,000?

Warm-Up/Review

Play a quick math fact fluency practice game. Say a problem, such as *5 + 2*. Call on a student to answer. Have the student that correctly answered the problem say another problem, such as *4 + 3*, and choose the next person to answer. Continue in this manner until everyone has had a turn.

 Mini-Lesson

Materials: base ten blocks

1. Draw a place value chart on the board with columns for the ones and the tens. Give students base ten blocks so they can follow along as you model. Write *39 + 15* vertically in the chart. Explain, "When we add, it is important to line up digits correctly—ones with ones and tens with tens."

2. Say, "When I add *9 + 5*, it equals 14, but there is only room for 1 digit." Demonstrate the concept of regrouping with the base ten blocks. Put 9 cubes and 5 cubes together. Then, count the total. (14) Say, "I can trade 10 cubes for a tens rod and still have 14." Count the blocks to confirm. "I write the 4 in the ones column because there are 4 cubes. Then, I carry the tens rod over to the tens column."

3. Point to the tens column. Explain, "I have 3 tens, 1 ten, and 1 ten for a total of 5 tens." Write *5* in the correct place.

4. Continue with other equations that require regrouping.

 Math Talk

Can you solve this in a different way?
How can you check your sum?
Why does regrouping work?

 Journal Prompt

Explain what *regrouping* (or *carrying*) means.
Give an example in your explanation.

Materials

base ten blocks
laminated place value charts
dry-erase markers

 Workstations

Activity sheets (pages 65–67)
Spin and Add (page 68)

 Guided Math

⭕ **Remediation: Hands-On Adding**

1. Give students laminated place value charts and dry-erase markers.
2. Write *29 + 24* to show students how to line up the problem by ones and tens. As you place base ten blocks, say, "The first number is 39, which has 3 tens and 9 ones; the second number has 2 tens and 4 ones." Have students count cubes along with you.
3. Say, "First, I add the ones column, 9 + 4." Place all of the cubes together and count them. "Because I can't put the number 13 in the ones column, I trade 10 cubes for a tens rod. Now, I have 3 cubes left and 1 tens rod. I write 3 in the ones column. Then, I carry the tens rod to the tens column."
4. As you add the tens, explain, "2 tens + 2 tens + 1 ten = 5 tens." Have students count their own blocks with you and write the results in the appropriate columns. Ask students to read their sums. Read the entire equation, pointing to each addend and the sum.
5. Continue practicing with equations that require regrouping.

⬜ **On Level: Carrying More Than Once**

1. Write *2,789 + 3,678.* (6,467) Complete the problem in front of the group, asking students to talk you through it as you work. Ask, "What column do I add first? 9 + 8 equals 17. Can I put a 2-digit number in the ones column? Which digit do I write in the ones column and which in the tens column?"
2. Continue, "In the tens place, I add 8 tens + 7 tens + 1 ten. That equals 16. Can I put a 2-digit number in the tens column? Which digit do I write in the tens column and which in the hundreds column? In the hundreds column, I add 7 hundreds + 6 hundreds + 1 hundred, which equals 14 hundreds." Question students to have them help you regroup again.
3. Finish with the thousands column.
4. Continue with other numbers that require more than one regrouping. Ask students to try the problems on their own and check their work together.

⚠️ **Enrichment: Is This Right?**

1. Write *3,412 + 4,538 = 7,940.* Tell students that you need their help. You know the problem is wrong. But, you don't know where the mistake is. Have students work through the problem and identify the mistake.
2. Discuss students' findings. "In the ones column, 8 + 2 = 10. The 0 was placed correctly in the ones column, but the ten was not carried to the tens column."
3. Continue with similar problems, such as *1,424 + 6,976 = 8,300.* Or, have students create problems for the group to solve.

 Assess and Extend

Have students solve the following problem: *Shane sells tickets to events at his school. So far, he has sold 1,321 adult tickets and 279 children's tickets for the football game. How many tickets has Shane sold for the football game?* (1,600)

Name _____   Date _____

Addition within 1,000   ⬤ Hands-On Adding

Solve each problem. Show your work.

1. 67
    + 23

2. 76
    + 5

3. 57
    + 16

4. 35
    + 25

5. 64
    + 18

6. 48
    + 22

7. 45
    + 30

8. 58
    + 19

9. 43
    + 14

10. 79
     + 4

11. 45
     + 29

12. 67
     + 13

13. 79
     + 16

14. 98
     + 1

15. 73
     + 17

16. 75
     + 10

17. 28
     + 19

18. 64
     + 17

19. 38
     + 29

20. 21
     + 19

Addition within 1,000   ■ Carrying More Than Once

Solve each problem. Show your work.

1.   362
      + 199

2.   414
      + 397

3.   655
      + 298

4.   515
      + 225

5.   198
      + 44

6.   609
      + 91

7.   724
      + 91

8.   457
      + 111

9.   672
      + 148

10.   484
      + 348

11. 3,459
      + 1,923

12. 6,410
      + 3,190

13. 8,009
      + 1,498

14. 4,852
      + 4,167

15. 4,444
      + 2,066

16. 3,471
      + 1,748

17. 5,617
      + 2,527

18. 9,411
      + 254

19. 6,240
      + 1,789

20. 7,019
      + 1,942

Addition within 1,000   ▲ Is This Right?

Check the problems below. If the problem is correct, draw a star next to the problem. If the problem is incorrect, show the mistake and solve the problem correctly.

1.
```
   6,175   _____
 + 1,268   _____
 --------
   7,333   _____
```

2.
```
   9,481   _____
 +   292   _____
 --------
   9,673   _____
```

3.
```
   1,542   _____
 + 4,810   _____
 --------
   6,352   _____
```

4.
```
  81,276   _____
 + 19,484  _____
 --------
  90,750   _____
```

5.
```
  47,528   _____
 + 13,561  _____
 --------
  60,089   _____
```

6.
```
  20,451   _____
 + 70,769  _____
 --------
  91,220   _____
```

7.
```
  48,152   _____
 +  1,940  _____
 --------
  49,092   _____
```

8.
```
  64,591   _____
 + 31,655  _____
 --------
  95,146   _____
```

9.
```
   7,900   _____
 + 4,150   _____
 --------
  12,050   _____
```

10.
```
  52,578   _____
 +  9,412  _____
 --------
  51,980   _____
```

Spin and Add

Materials: sharpened pencil, paper clip

To play: Use the pencil and paper clip to spin each spinner. Use the numbers to create an addition problem. Record it in the space below. Then, solve.

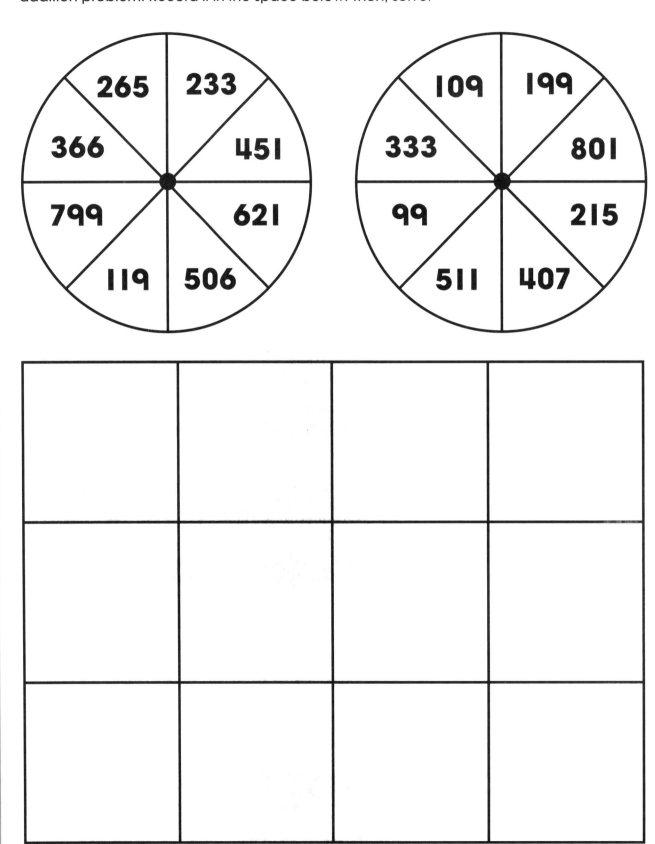

© Carson-Dellosa • CD-104955

Essential Question

How can strategies and step-by-step methods help with subtraction within 1,000?

Warm-Up/Review

Review regrouping by reviewing how to add numbers that require regrouping. Use the following problems: 645 – 209 (436); 231 – 102 (129); 852 – 658 (194).

 Mini-Lesson

Materials: base ten blocks

1. Write *90 – 13* on the board. Show the class 9 tens rods.

2. Say, "I want to take away 13 from this 90. I can take 10 (1 ten) but right now, there aren't any ones to subtract the 3. So, I have to ungroup, or borrow, 1 of the tens from 90." Demonstrate trading a tens rod from the group of 9 tens for 10 cubes. Count the rods and the cubes to confirm that they still total 90.

3. Show the process on the equation. Say, "I'm going to cross off the 9 and write an 8 above it because I ungrouped 1 of the tens and have 8 tens left. Then, I cross off the 0 and write a 10 above it because I now have 10 ones."

4. Take away 3 ones and 1 ten. Ask students to help count how many are left. (77) Record the answer and read the complete equation.

5. Have students work independently on the problem *51 – 36*. (15) Observe any mistakes that students make. Teach to those mistakes and correct the problems together.

 Math Talk

Can you check your subtraction problem? Is there another way to solve a subtraction problem?
Explain how and why you regrouped here.

 Journal Prompt

Explain the difference between regrouping during addition and subtraction. Then, tell how they are similar.

Materials

base ten blocks

 Workstations

Activity sheets (pages 71–73)
Puzzling Subtraction (page 74)

 Guided Math

⊙ **Remediation: Hands-On Subtracting**

1. Provide students with base ten blocks. Write *60 – 22*. Say, "We start the problem with 60 blocks—6 tens and 0 ones." Count 6 tens rods with students.

2. Say, "Then, it says to take away 22. How many tens and ones are in 22? Can you take away the tens? The ones? Because I can't break these rods, I have to ungroup 1 of the tens." Take 1 tens rod and trade it for 10 cubes. After the trade, count all of the rods and cubes to show that they still total 60.

3. Demonstrate the process on the equation. Explain, "I ungrouped 1 of the tens. That left me with 5 tens." Cross off the 6 and write *5* above it. "I started with 0 ones, and now I have 10." Cross off the 0 and write *10* above it. Take away 2 of the ones and 2 tens, and record the solution. (38)

4. Continue with other equations that require ungrouping.

⬜ **On Level: Borrowing More Than Once**

1. Write *500 – 79*. Draw 5 squares to represent 5 hundreds. Have students copy the problem and picture.

2. Say, "Start with 500. We need to subtract 9 ones and 7 tens. Because we don't have any ones, go to the tens. Are there any tens? Where do we go next? Because there are no tens, ungroup 1 of the hundreds into 10 tens." With students, cross off 1 of the square blocks and draw 10 lines to represent tens rods. Show on the equation that there are 4 hundreds and 10 tens.

3. Say, "Now ungroup 1 of the tens into 10 ones." In your drawing, represent the cubes with dots. Show in the problem that there are now 9 tens and 10 ones. Count to confirm that the total is still 500.

4. Have students subtract 7 tens and 9 ones. Write the results on the equation. (421) Read the complete equation.

5. Continue with other equations that require multiple ungroupings.

△ **Enrichment: Estimating to Mentally Subtract**

1. Write *4,000 – 2,175*. Have students estimate the answer. Ask, "What did you round 2,175 to in order to estimate? How does rounding to the nearest hundred make it easier to mentally subtract?"

2. Now, have students find the exact answer. (1,825) Compare their estimates to the exact answer. Ask, "How do they compare? What happens if we estimate to the nearest ten? Does that make it easier or more difficult to mentally calculate the answer?"

3. Demonstrate using estimation to find the exact answer to the problem above. Say, "I know I need 825 to round 2,175 to 3,000 (2,175 + 825 = 3,000). Then, I need 1,000 to get from 3,000 to 4,000 (3,000 + 1,000 = 4,000). Adding these numbers gives me the answer of 1,825 (1,000 + 825 = 1,825)."

4. Continue with other equations, having students explain their estimation thought processes.

 Assess and Extend

Have students solve the following problem: *Grey works at an ice-cream shop. On Thursday, he sold 234 scoops of ice cream and on Friday he sold 709 scoops of ice cream. Over the weekend, Grey sold 980 scoops of ice cream. How many more scoops did Grey sell during the weekend than he did on Thursday and Friday?* (37)

Subtraction within 1,000   ● Hands-On Subtracting

Solve each problem. Use base ten blocks to help you. Show your work.

1. $\begin{array}{r} 4\,0 \\ -\,1\,4 \\ \hline \end{array}$

2. $\begin{array}{r} 2\,0 \\ -\ \ 9 \\ \hline \end{array}$

3. $\begin{array}{r} 9\,0 \\ -\,2\,5 \\ \hline \end{array}$

4. $\begin{array}{r} 7\,0 \\ -\,6\,2 \\ \hline \end{array}$

5. $\begin{array}{r} 3\,0 \\ -\,2\,2 \\ \hline \end{array}$

6. $\begin{array}{r} 5\,0 \\ -\,3\,3 \\ \hline \end{array}$

7. $\begin{array}{r} 8\,0 \\ -\,6\,9 \\ \hline \end{array}$

8. $\begin{array}{r} 7\,0 \\ -\,1\,5 \\ \hline \end{array}$

9. $\begin{array}{r} 6\,0 \\ -\,4\,1 \\ \hline \end{array}$

10. $\begin{array}{r} 2\,0 \\ -\,1\,6 \\ \hline \end{array}$

11. $\begin{array}{r} 9\,0 \\ -\,5\,7 \\ \hline \end{array}$

12. $\begin{array}{r} 4\,0 \\ -\,2\,8 \\ \hline \end{array}$

13. $\begin{array}{r} 5\,0 \\ -\,3\,6 \\ \hline \end{array}$

14. $\begin{array}{r} 8\,0 \\ -\,7\,7 \\ \hline \end{array}$

15. $\begin{array}{r} 6\,0 \\ -\,1\,4 \\ \hline \end{array}$

16. $\begin{array}{r} 3\,0 \\ -\,1\,8 \\ \hline \end{array}$

17. $\begin{array}{r} 5\,0 \\ -\,3\,9 \\ \hline \end{array}$

18. $\begin{array}{r} 4\,0 \\ -\,1\,0 \\ \hline \end{array}$

19. $\begin{array}{r} 7\,0 \\ -\,1\,3 \\ \hline \end{array}$

20. $\begin{array}{r} 8\,0 \\ -\,4\,2 \\ \hline \end{array}$

Subtraction within 1,000 ■ Borrowing More Than Once

Solve each problem. Draw a picture to show your work.

1.   30
      − 18

2.   90
      − 22

3.   40
      − 11

4.   80
      − 35

5.   70
      − 46

6.   400
      − 23

7.   500
      − 124

8.   900
      − 368

9.   700
      − 414

10.   800
       − 350

11. 6,000
       − 1,400

12. 8,000
       − 2,042

13. 3,000
       − 1,243

14. 2,000
       − 24

15. 9,000
       − 409

16. 1,000
       − 421

Name _____   Date _____

First, estimate each answer. Then, solve.

1.   400
           − 196

Estimate: _____

Actual: _____

2.   600
           − 241

Estimate: _____

Actual: _____

3.   800
           − 95

Estimate: _____

Actual: _____

4.   200
           − 45

Estimate: _____

Actual: _____

5.   6,000
           − 3,228

Estimate: _____

Actual: _____

6.   2,000
           − 850

Estimate: _____

Actual: _____

7.   3,000
           − 2,040

Estimate: _____

Actual: _____

8.   7,000
           − 4,727

Estimate: _____

Actual: _____

9.   20,000
           − 854

Estimate: _____

Actual: _____

10.   80,000
           − 24,043

Estimate: _____

Actual: _____

11.   60,000
           − 34,216

Estimate: _____

Actual: _____

12.   10,000
           − 894

Estimate: _____

Actual: _____

13.   50,000
           − 43

Estimate: _____

Actual: _____

14.   70,000
           − 44,444

Estimate: _____

Actual: _____

15.   60,000
           − 9,423

Estimate: _____

Actual: _____

Puzzling Subtraction

Directions: Align edges with matching expressions and differences. All pieces will be used. If a piece doesn't fit, or if an answer seems to be missing, at least one piece is placed incorrectly.

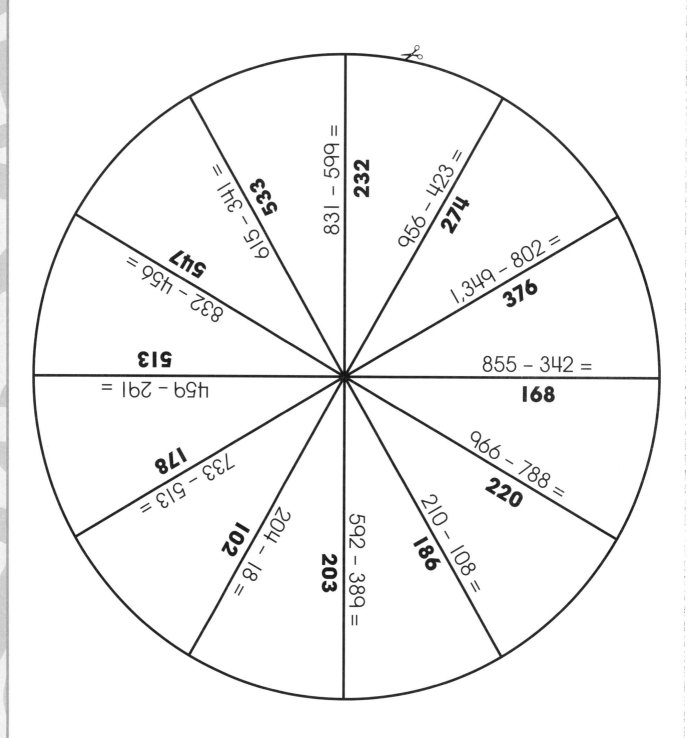

To prep: If desired, print on card stock and laminate for durability. Cut on the solid lines to separate the pieces. Make several sets on different colors of card stock.

74   © Carson-Dellosa • CD-104955

Multiplying with Multiples of 10

 Essential Question

What strategies help with multiplying 1-digit numbers by multiples of 10?

 Warm-Up/Review

Write *2 x 10* on the board. Review with students how to skip count by 10s. Say, "Since students have 10 fingers each, how many fingers do 2 students have? (20) Five students? (50) Ten students? (100) Our whole class?"

 Mini-Lesson

Materials: base ten blocks, 0–9 number cards

1. Write *3 x 40* on the board. Say, "How can you make 40 using groups of 10?" Demonstrate with base ten blocks using 4 rods. Write *40 = 4 x 10* on the board.

2. Ask students, "How can you model all of the groups of 40?" Explain to students that they can add 2 more groups of 4 rods each. Model and have students do the same.

3. Count together by tens, rod by rod, to determine the total. Write the equation *3 x (4 x 10) = 120* on the board. Have students identify the repeated addition sentence for this problem also (40 + 40 + 40 = 120).

4. Ask, "Can you identify any patterns within the factors and products?" Direct them to see 3 x 4 = 12, and 3 x 40 = 120 are related. Point out that the 0 means they are multiplying by 10 times as much, so the product is also 10 times larger.

5. Give pairs of students a set of number cards. Have them write a blank multiplication sentence (__ x __ = __), pull out the zero, and place it at the end of the second factor. Then, students should take turns drawing two cards and placing them in the number sentence. So, drawing a 2 and a 5 would create the problem 2 x 50. Solve and repeat.

 Math Talk

Could this problem be solved another way? How?

Which property of multiplication may help with solving this problem?

Why would it be helpful to break up the multiple of 10?

 Journal Prompt

Explain why 3 groups of 40 is the same as 12 groups of 10. You may draw a model to help you.

Materials

base ten blocks

 Workstations

Activity sheets (pages 77–79)
Multiples of 10 Poke Cards
(page 80)

 Guided Math

⚪ **Remediation: Using Base Ten Blocks**

1. Write *20 × 4*.
2. Say, "We start the problem by making a group of 20 with tens rods." Count out 2 tens rods with students. Have students model the problem with base ten rods like in the Mini-Lesson (page 75). Count together by tens, rod by rod to determine the total.
3. Write the equations *4 × 20 = 80* and *4 × (2 × 10) = 80*. Explain that 20, 4 times, is 2 tens rods repeated 4 times. Write *20 + 20 + 20 + 20 = 80* and say, "This is the repeated addition sentence for the problem *4 × 20 = 80*."
4. Have students continue practicing using base ten blocks to solve similar problems.

🟦 **On Level: Solving Multiple Ways**

1. Write *60 × 5*. Ask students to use their own methods to solve the problem. Have students share their answers and strategies.
2. First, write *60* five times and add. Next demonstrate how to use the grid or lattice method and calculate 60 × 5.
3. Use mental math. Explain that since there is one 0 at the end of 60, there will be a 0 at the end of our product. Say, "So, we multiply 6 × 5 and get 30. We add one 0 to the end (because we are actually multiplying by 6 tens, not 6) and we have the answer of 300."
4. Have students practice the various methods with additional similar problems.

🔺 **Enrichment: Working with Larger Numbers**

1. Write *400 × 7*. Ask students to solve the problem independently.
2. Ask students to first recognize that the two 0s at the end of 400 mean that there will be two 0s at the end of the product because we are multiplying by 4 hundreds, not 4. Say, "We multiply 4 × 7 to get 28, and add the two 0s to the end of our product to get 2,800."
3. Now, write *800 × 3*. Have students solve the problem and explain how they get to the answer.
4. Have students continue practicing with additional problems, including problems like 210 × 2. (420)

 Assess and Extend

Have students solve the following problem: *Kennedy bought a bundle of sticky notes. In the bundle were 8 smaller packages, and in each of those packages were 3 packs of 10 pads of sticky notes. To find the total number of sticky note pads she bought, Kennedy wrote this equation: 30 × 8 = 240. Is she correct? Explain how you know.* (Yes)

Multiplying with Multiples of 10 ● Using Base Ten Blocks

Draw base ten blocks to model the problem. Then, solve.

1. 30 × 4 =

2. 10 × 8 =

3. 20 × 6 =

4. 20 × 9 =

5. 40 × 9 =

6. 30 × 7 =

7. 50 × 4 =

8. 40 × 6 =

9. 80 × 7 =

10. 50 × 5 =

11. 40 × 3 =

12. 60 × 4 =

13. 10 × 9 =

14. 70 × 3 =

15. 60 × 2 =

16. 80 × 2 =

Multiplying with Multiples of 10   ■ Solving Multiple Ways

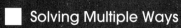

Solve each problem. Show your work. Demonstrate the method you used to solve.

I. 90 × 3 =   **2.** 70 × 9 =

3. 80 × 4 =   **4.** 60 × 8 =

5. 70 × 5 =   **6.** 50 × 3 =

7. 60 × 6 =   **8.** 40 × 6 =

9. 50 × 7 =   **10.** 30 × 5 =

II. 40 × 8 =   **12.** 20 × 4 =

13. 30 × 9 =   **14.** 10 × 3 =

15. 20 × 2 =   **16.** 80 × 9 =

Multiplying with Multiples of 10   ▲ Working with Larger Numbers

Solve each problem. Show your work.

1. 900 × 5 =   **2.** 600 × 9 =

3. 800 × 4 =   **4.** 400 × 5 =

5. 700 × 3 =   **6.** 300 × 6 =

7. 600 × 2 =   **8.** 600 × 6 =

9. 500 × 6 =   **10.** 800 × 5 =

11. 400 × 7 =   **12.** 700 × 7 =

13. 300 × 8 =   **14.** 800 × 9 =

15. 220 × 3 =   **16.** 410 × 2 =

Multiples of 10 Poke Cards

Directions: Choose a card, find the missing number, and then poke a pencil through the hole you think is the correct answer. To check, turn the card over to see if the pencil is inserted through the circled hole.

2 × 20			**3 × 30**		
40	50	60	60	90	100
●	●	●	●	●	●

5 × 70			**6 × 40**		
300	400	350	210	240	260
●	●	●	●	●	●

8 × 50			**9 × 60**		
450	400	480	320	600	540
●	●	●	●	●	●

4 × 80			**7 × 90**		
360	320	400	600	630	700
●	●	●	●	●	●

20 × 9			**30 × 8**		
180	810	80	320	240	300
●	●	●	●	●	●

40 × 7			**50 × 6**		
200	260	280	350	340	300
●	●	●	●	●	●

60 × 5			**70 × 4**		
280	300	350	280	240	300
●	●	●	●	●	●

80 × 3			**90 × 2**		
240	270	290	800	160	180
●	●	●	●	●	●

To prep: If desired, print on card stock. Cut out the cards and laminate them for durability. Use a hole punch to punch holes over the black circles on each card. Then, use a permanent marker to circle the correct hole on the back of the card.

Understanding Fractions

 Essential Question

How do fractions show parts
of a whole?
What are numerators and
denominators?

 Warm-Up/Review

Read the book *Fraction Action* by Loreen
Leedy (Holiday House, 1994) or another
picture book about fractions.

 Mini-Lesson

Materials: index cards

1. Draw a circle on the board. Say, "This circle can be used to represent 1 whole. We can partition this circle into equal parts." Divide the circle into 2 halves. Say, "This circle has been partitioned into 2 equal parts, or halves."

2. Draw 2 more circles. Divide one circle into thirds and one into fourths to demonstrate 3 equal parts and 4 equal parts.

3. Shade in 1 part of the circle divided in half. Say, "We can shade a portion of a circle to name a specific part of the whole. The shaded portion of this circle is one-half of the whole." Shade 2 parts of the circle divided into thirds and 1 part of the circle divided into fourths to show two-thirds and one-fourth.

4. Say, "The numbers 1/2, 2/3 and 1/4 are called *fractions*. A fraction names an equal part of an area or part of a group. The top number of the fraction is called the *numerator*. It tells how many of the total parts are being counted. The bottom number is called the *denominator*. It counts how many total equal parts a shape or figure is partitioned into."

5. Give each student an index card. Have them fold it in half, and in half again. When they open it back up, have them draw lines along the folds, shade 2 parts of the index card, and write the fraction of the card they shaded. (2/4)

6. Draw a circle divided into unequal fourths with 1 part shaded. Discuss with the class why this is or is not an appropriate fraction.

7. Continue practicing showing fractions and non-fractions using different shapes. Have students identify whether each is a fraction, and if so, which fraction is shown.

 Math Talk

What does the numerator tell you in a
fraction? Denominator?
What could this fraction describe?
Describe a real-world example of when you
would use/see a fraction.

 Journal Prompt

Draw several models
showing the fraction 1/2
using different shapes.

Materials

pattern blocks
graph paper
two-color counters

 Workstations

Activity sheets (pages 83–85)
Fraction Match-Up (page 86)

 Guided Math

⭕ **Remediation: Fraction Models**

1. Show students a yellow hexagon pattern block. Say, "This yellow hexagon is equal to 1 whole." Next, show rhombuses, triangles, and trapezoids.
2. Show students how 2 trapezoids can cover the whole hexagon, therefore 1 trapezoid is 1/2 of the whole hexagon.
3. Give each student a hexagon and enough rhombuses, triangles, and trapezoids. Have them experiment with the shapes to determine which fractional part a rhombus is and a triangle is of the whole hexagon.
4. Extend their practice further by having students determine what fraction a triangle is of a rhombus and of a trapezoid (1/2 and 1/3).

🔲 **On Level: Understanding Larger Fractions**

1. Draw a square. Divide the square into 4 equal parts. Ask, "How many parts have I divided this whole into?" Shade 1 part of the square. Ask, "What fraction of the whole is shaded?" (1/4)
2. Draw a rectangle. Divide it into 7 equal parts. Shade 3 parts. Ask, "What fraction of this whole is shaded?" (3/7)
3. Have students practice with other fractions by drawing them on graph paper and coloring in the appropriate shaded portions: 4/10, 2/5, 3/3, 5/8. Each time, have students write the fraction that is shaded.

🔺 **Enrichment: Fractions of a Set**

1. Write the fraction *1/3*. Have students draw a picture to model 1/3.
2. Say, "Let's suppose I had 3 whole pizzas. Another way to show 1/3 is to show parts of a set. In this set of 3 whole pizzas, 1/3 would be 1 whole pizza—1 whole pizza out of a set of 3 whole pizzas."
3. Show another example with 1/4 and 4 brownies.
4. Continue to practice with parts of a set and other fractions. Give students pattern blocks and two-color counters to allow them to follow along and show the fractions of a set. Then, have students move toward drawing examples of fractions of a set.

 Assess and Extend

Have students solve the following problem: *There are 2 blue water balloons, 5 red water balloons, and 4 yellow water balloons in a box. What fraction of the water balloons are red or yellow?* (5/11, 4/11) *If the number of water balloons of each color in the box was doubled, how would your answer change?* (10/22, 8/22)

1/4 Understanding Fractions   ● Fraction Models

Write the fraction that describes the shaded part of each whole.

1.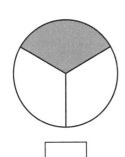

2.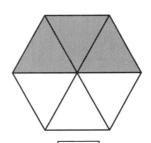

3.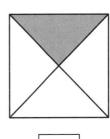

4.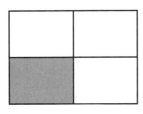

5.

6.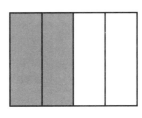

7.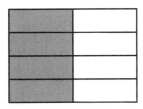

8.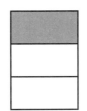

9.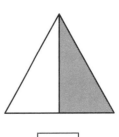

10.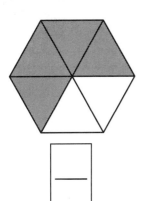

11.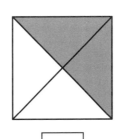

12.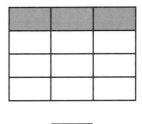

¼ Understanding Fractions   ☐ Understanding Larger Fractions

Shade to show each fraction.

1.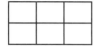

$$\frac{4}{6}$$

2.

$$\frac{3}{8}$$

3.

$$\frac{2}{3}$$

4.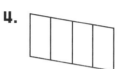

$$\frac{1}{4}$$

5.

$$\frac{1}{3}$$

6.

$$\frac{2}{4}$$

7.

$$\frac{3}{6}$$

8.

$$\frac{3}{8}$$

9.

$$\frac{2}{4}$$

10.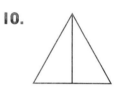

$$\frac{1}{2}$$

11.

$$\frac{1}{4}$$

12.

$$\frac{2}{6}$$

13.

$$\frac{3}{4}$$

14.

$$\frac{1}{3}$$

15.

$$\frac{5}{6}$$

16.

$$\frac{4}{6}$$

17.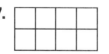

$$\frac{6}{8}$$

18.

$$\frac{1}{6}$$

19.

$$\frac{4}{8}$$

20.

$$\frac{2}{4}$$

¼ Understanding Fractions ▲ Fractions of a Set

Write the fraction of each set that is shaded.

1.

2.

3.

4.

5.

6.

7.

8.

9.

10.

Draw a fraction of a set that shows each fraction below.

11. $\dfrac{2}{8}$

12. $\dfrac{1}{5}$

13. $\dfrac{1}{2}$

14. $\dfrac{3}{12}$

15. $\dfrac{5}{8}$

16. $\dfrac{4}{6}$

Fraction Match-Up

To play: Shuffle the cards. Place them facedown in a 4 by 4 grid. Players take turns flipping over 2 cards at a time, trying to match a fraction with a fraction model. After all of the cards have been matched, the player with the most card pairs wins.

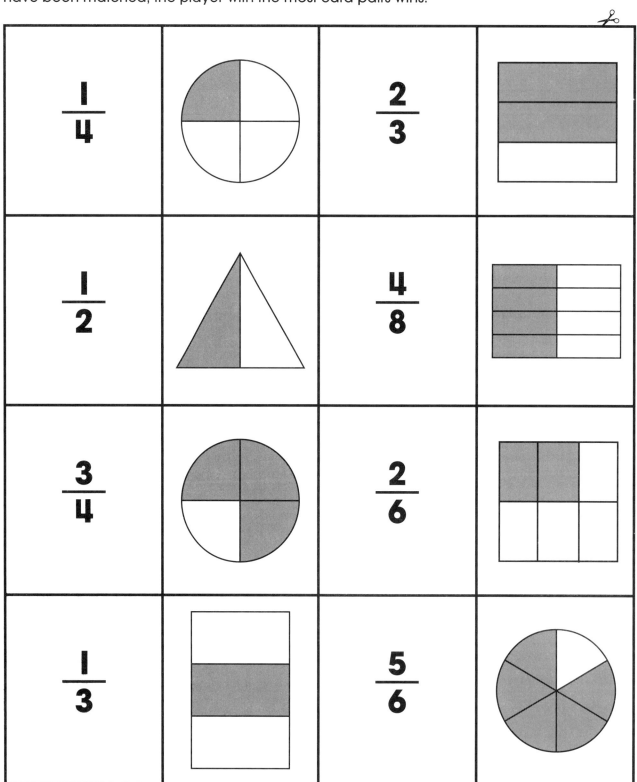

To prep: If desired, print on card stock and laminate for durability. Cut on the solid lines to separate the pieces. Make several sets by copying on different colors of card stock.

Fractions on a Number Line

 Essential Question

How can fractions be represented on a number line?

 Warm-Up/Review

Have a certain number of students come to the front of the class. Ask students to identify the fraction for the number of students who are girls; are wearing red; are wearing blue jeans; etc. Choose different things specific to the class and have students identify the fraction of students each time.

 Mini-Lesson

Materials: laminated blank number lines, dry-erase markers

1. Draw a number line on the board. Mark and label the numbers *0*, *1*, and *2*. Say, "A fraction shows parts of a whole, therefore each part is more than 0, but less than 1 whole. I am going to divide my number line between 0 and 1 into 4 equal sections to show fourths." Model this for students.

2. Point to the first mark and ask, "What should I label this section? Since we have 4 equal sections and we are moving 1 section closer to the number 1, we have moved forward 1 out of 4 sections, or 1/4." Label the first mark *1/4*.

3. Explain to students how to label the next 2 marks on the number line as 2/4 and 3/4. Then, explain how to label 4/4 where 1 is and explain the relationship between 4/4 and 1 whole.

4. Give students laminated blank number lines and have them practice dividing the number lines into different fractions, such as halves, thirds, fifths, sixths, eighths, etc. Have students label each section of the number line with the appropriate fractions.

 Math Talk

Why is it important for each section on the number line to be equal?
Explain why 4/4 and 1 whole are equal.
What does it mean when 2 fractions share the same mark, such as 1/2 and 2/4?

 Journal Prompt

Draw and label the following fractions on a number line: *1/8, 2/8, 3/8, 4/8, 5/8, 6/8, 7/8, 8/8*

Materials

laminated blank number lines
dry-erase markers

 Workstations

Activity sheets (pages 89–91)
Fraction Number Line Task Cards
(page 92)

 Guided Math

○ **Remediation: Understanding Number Lines**

1. Draw a number line divided into 3 sections with 0 and 1 labeled. Ask, "How many parts is this number line divided into? (3) What fraction does each section of the number line represent?" (1/3) Emphasize that the entire space between the tick marks is what represents the fractional part, not the tick mark itself.
2. Demonstrate how to label the number line with the correct fractions.
3. Ask, "Where would I put the fraction 2/3?" Draw a dot and label it *2/3*.
4. Give each student a laminated blank number line. Have them practice with other fractions and answer the same questions as in step 1 and step 3.

▢ **On Level: Identifying Fractions**

1. Draw a number line divided into sixths. Label each mark dividing the number line with a dot and a letter, *A, B, C, D,* or *E*.
2. Ask, "Which dot shows the location of 1/6? 5/6?" Give students a laminated blank number line and have them copy the number line drawn in step 1 and label all of the fractions on the number line.
3. Have students draw a dot to represent the fraction 6/6 and label it with the letter *F*. Have students explain where 6/6 goes on the number line and why.
4. Have students practice drawing other fractions on the number line and answer similar questions as in step 2.

△ **Enrichment: Representing Fractions**

1. Draw a blank number line that has a mark for 0 and 1, but is otherwise unlabeled. Write the fraction *2/6*. Have students draw the number line. Say, "Show this fraction on the number line."
2. Assist students with first dividing the number line into 6 equal parts. Discuss how to start at the beginning and count forward to get to the fraction 2/6.
3. Practice with other fractions, having students draw the number line, divide it into parts, and label a specific fraction.

 Assess and Extend

Display the following number lines. Tell students, "These number lines are divided into eighths. Identify the correct number line and explain why the other one is incorrect."

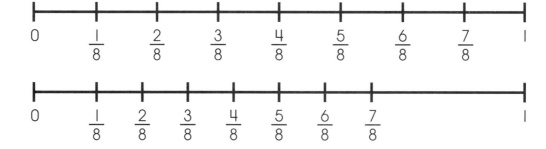

Name _____   Date _____

¼ **Fractions on a Number Line**   ● Understanding Number Lines

Use the number lines to answer the questions.

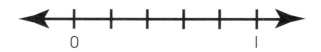

0   1

1. The number line is divided into _____ parts.

2. Label the number line with the correct fractions.

3. Each section of the number line represents what fraction? _____

4. Draw a dot to show the location of $\frac{3}{5}$.

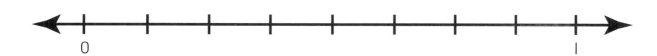

0   1

5. The number line is divided into _____ parts.

6. Label the number line with the correct fractions.

7. Each section of the number line represents what fraction? _____

8. Draw a dot to show the location of $\frac{7}{8}$.

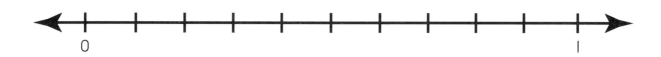

0   1

9. The number line is divided into _____ parts.

10. Label the number line with the correct fractions.

11. Each section of the number line represents what fraction? _____

12. Draw a dot to show the location of $\frac{5}{10}$.

¼ Fractions on a Number Line   ☐ Identifying Fractions

Use the number lines to answer the questions.

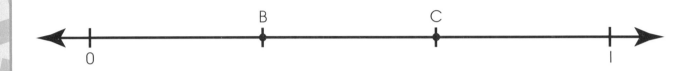

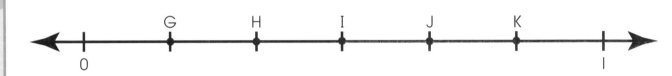

1. Label each number line with the correct fractions.

2. Which dot shows the location of $\frac{1}{3}$? _____

3. Which dot shows the location of $\frac{1}{4}$? _____

4. Which dot shows the location of $\frac{4}{6}$? _____

5. Which dot shows the location of $\frac{1}{2}$? _____

6. Which dot shows the location of $\frac{2}{6}$? _____

7. Which dot shows the location of $\frac{3}{4}$? _____

8. Choose a fraction represented on a number line above. Draw a different representation of it.

Name _____   Date _____

¼ Fractions on a Number Line   ▲ Representing Fractions

Show each fraction on the number line.

1. $\dfrac{2}{6}$ ←─┼────────────────────┼─→	**2.** $\dfrac{2}{4}$ ←─┼───────────────────────┼─→
3. $\dfrac{5}{6}$ ←─┼────────────────────┼─→	**4.** $\dfrac{4}{7}$ ←─┼────────────────────┼─→
5. $\dfrac{3}{3}$ ←─┼────────────────────┼─→	**6.** $\dfrac{2}{5}$ ←─┼───────────────────────┼─→
7. $\dfrac{1}{2}$ ←─┼────────────────────┼─→	**8.** $\dfrac{3}{4}$ ←─┼───────────────────────┼─→
9. $\dfrac{4}{4}$ ←─┼────────────────────┼─→	**10.** $\dfrac{5}{5}$ ←─┼───────────────────────┼─→

Fraction Number Line Task Cards

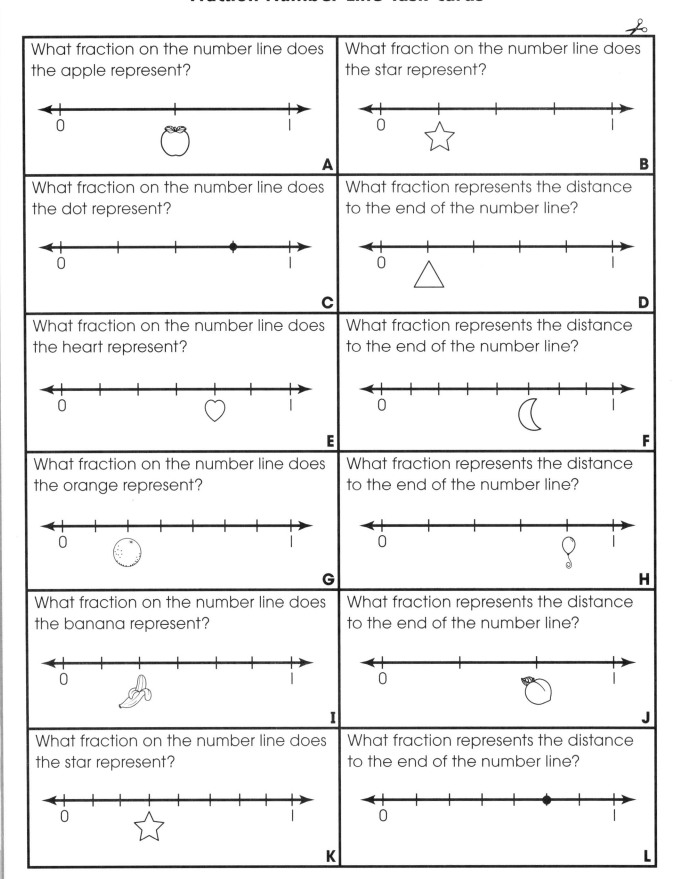

What fraction on the number line does the apple represent?

0   1

A

What fraction on the number line does the star represent?

0   1

B

What fraction on the number line does the dot represent?

0   1

C

What fraction represents the distance to the end of the number line?

0   1

D

What fraction on the number line does the heart represent?

0   1

E

What fraction represents the distance to the end of the number line?

0   1

F

What fraction on the number line does the orange represent?

0   1

G

What fraction represents the distance to the end of the number line?

0   1

H

What fraction on the number line does the banana represent?

0   1

I

What fraction represents the distance to the end of the number line?

0   1

J

What fraction on the number line does the star represent?

0   1

K

What fraction represents the distance to the end of the number line?

0   1

L

To prep: If desired, copy the task cards on card stock for durability. Laminate the cards so students can use dry-erase markers.

 **Equivalent Fractions**

? Essential Question

How can equivalent fractions be identified using visual models and number lines?

Warm-Up/Review

Show or draw pictures of the following: a chocolate bar divided into eighths, a football field divided into tenths, a pizza divided into 8 slices, etc. Have students identify half of each object that you display.

Note: Save the pictures to use in the mini-lesson.

★ Mini-Lesson

Materials: pictures used in the warm-up/review section

1. Draw a circle divided in half with 1 part shaded next to a circle divided into fourths with 2 parts shaded. Ask, "What fraction of each circle is shaded?" Students should say that the first circle shows 1/2 and the second shows 2/4.

2. Ask, "If this were 2 cookies, and you could either have 1/2 of this cookie, or 2/4 of this cookie, which would be the larger amount?" Students should see that both amounts are the same.

3. Explain that we can see by looking at the model that 1/2 and 2/4 are equal, or *equivalent*.

4. Draw a number line on the board with the top of the number line divided into halves and the bottom of the number line divided into fourths. Demonstrate the same relationship of 1/2 and 2/4 on a number line.

5. Continue modeling other equivalent fractions using models and number lines.

6. Have students look at the images from the warm-up activity. With a partner, they should identify the fractions equivalent to 1/2 shown in each image.

Math Talk

Can more than two fractions be equivalent? How do you know?

Why is it important for the parts of the whole and the parts of a number line to be equal in size?

Explain another way to show equivalent fractions.

Journal Prompt

Draw a model with 4 equal parts and one with 8 equal parts. Shade each model to show two equivalent fractions. Write the fractions. Explain how you know they are equal.

Materials

five strips of 3 x 18-inch construction
    paper (different colors)
fraction bars (optional)
scissors
envelopes
marker

 Workstations

Activity sheets (pages 95–97)
Equivalent Fraction Bump
    (page 98)

 Guided Math

○ Remediation: Hands-On Models

1. Give each student five different color strips of construction paper. Demonstrate how to take one strip and label it *1 whole*. With the second strip, have students fold it in half and cut along the fold. Label each half *1/2*. Continue modeling how to cut and create fraction bars for fourths and eighths.

2. Write *3/4*. Say, "Show me with your fraction bars how many eighths are equal to 3/4." Model how to first show 3/4. Then, line up as many eighths as are equal to 3/4. Then, count the eighths and write the equivalent fraction, *6/8*.

3. Have students continue practicing with other equivalent fractions, using only the fractions that they created earlier (halves, fourths, and eighths). If desired, give students copies of fraction bars to cut apart so students can work with thirds, sixths, etc.

▢ On Level: Using Other Methods

1. Write *1/2 = 3/6*. Have students draw models that show that 1/2 and 3/6 are equivalent. Allow students to share and compare their models,

2. Draw two number lines, one above the other. (It is important to keep them in line with each other.) Divide the top one in half and the bottom one into sixths, and label both number lines. Put a dot at 1/2 and a dot at 3/6. Explain, "We can show equivalent fractions on a number line as well." Emphasize the importance of equal parts and lining up the number lines.

3. Point to *1/2 = 3/6* again. Say, "We can also determine equivalent fractions by multiplying or dividing the numerators and denominators by the same number." Rewrite 1/2 and write × 3 = next to both the 1 and 2 . Ask, "What is 1 times 3? (3) What is 2 times 3? (6) Record 3/6 to the right of the =. Therefore, 1/2 = 3/6." Then, model dividing 3/6 by 3/3 to find the same answer.

4. Have students continue practicing with other equivalent fractions using models, number lines, and multiplication or division.

△ Enrichment: Prove It

1. Write *1/4* and *3/8*, side by side. Ask students, "Are these fractions equivalent? Prove it by using models, a number line, or multiplication or division."

2. Have students share their findings and explain why the fractions are or are not equivalent. For example, "1/4 and 3/8 are not equivalent because when I draw the number line for fourths and eighths, 1/4 and 3/8 do not fall at the same point."

3. Have students continue practicing with other fraction pairs, especially the larger fractions, such as tenths and twelfths. Encourage students to justify each comparison in some way.

 Assess and Extend

Have students solve the following problem: *Emily says that 5/8 and 1/2 are equivalent. Is she correct? How do you know? Explain with words and models.*

Name _____ Date _____

Write the equivalent fractions.

1.

____ = ____

2.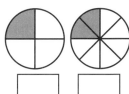

____ = ____

3.

____ = ____

4.

____ = ____

5.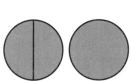

____ = ____

6.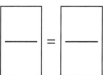

____ = ____

7.

____ = ____

8.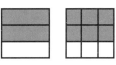

____ = ____

9.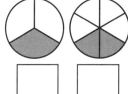

____ = ____

Write each fraction. Draw a line to connect the equivalent fractions.

10.

11.

12.

13.

14.

15.

Name _____   **Date** _____

 **Equivalent Fractions**   ☐ **Using Other Methods**

Write the equivalent fractions.

1. ←|——|——●——|——→   **2.** ←|——|——●——|——|——→   **3.** ←|——●——|——|——→
   0   1   0   1   0   1

←|—|—|—●—|—→   ←|—|—|—●—|—|—→   ←|—|—●—|—|—|—|—→
 0   1   0   1   0   1

☐ — = ☐ —   ☐ — = ☐ —   ☐ — = ☐ —

Find each equivalent fraction.

4. $\frac{1}{2} = \frac{\square}{4}$ **5.** $\frac{1}{3} = \frac{\square}{6}$ **6.** $\frac{3}{4} = \frac{\square}{8}$ **7.** $\frac{1}{2} = \frac{3}{\square}$ **8.** $\frac{2}{3} = \frac{4}{\square}$

9. $\frac{4}{8} = \frac{\square}{4}$ **10.** $\frac{2}{2} = \frac{3}{\square}$ **11.** $\frac{4}{6} = \frac{2}{\square}$ **12.** $\frac{4}{4} = \frac{2}{\square}$ **13.** $\frac{1}{3} = \frac{\square}{6}$

14. Choose two equivalent fractions from problems 4–8. Draw a picture to show how they are equivalent.

15. Choose two equivalent fractions from problems 9–13. Use number lines to show how they are equivalent.

96   © Carson-Dellosa • CD-104955

¼ Equivalent Fractions ▲ Prove It

Decide if each pair of fractions is equivalent. Draw an X on the pairs that are not equivalent. Draw a picture for each pair to explain why or why not.

1. $\frac{2}{4}$ and $\frac{2}{6}$

2. $\frac{2}{3}$ and $\frac{2}{4}$

3. $\frac{4}{8}$ and $\frac{1}{2}$

4. $\frac{2}{6}$ and $\frac{4}{12}$

5. $\frac{1}{2}$ and $\frac{3}{6}$

6. $\frac{3}{10}$ and $\frac{7}{12}$

7. $\frac{3}{4}$ and $\frac{2}{3}$

8. $\frac{3}{3}$ and $\frac{4}{4}$

9. $\frac{2}{4}$ and $\frac{5}{10}$

Equivalent Fraction Bump

Materials: 2 dice, 10 two-color counters per player, 2 counters to move around the board

To play: Players take turns. Place a counter on Start for each player. Roll the dice and move that many spaces. Match the fraction model you landed on to an equivalent model in the center of the board. Player 2 confirms whether player 1 has identified an equivalent fraction correctly. If correct, player 1 can cover the equivalent model with a counter. If incorrect, player 2 takes a turn. You can "bump" the other player off a space if they have only 1 counter on it. Once you place 2 counters on a space, it is yours and cannot be bumped. The first player to use all of her counters wins.

Start →	$\frac{3}{4}$	$\frac{1}{3}$	$\frac{2}{5}$	$\frac{1}{2}$	$\frac{2}{8}$
$\frac{8}{10}$					$\frac{8}{8}$
$\frac{4}{8}$					$\frac{2}{10}$
$\frac{2}{10}$					$\frac{8}{10}$
$\frac{2}{8}$					$\frac{2}{3}$
$\frac{2}{5}$	$\frac{1}{3}$	$\frac{3}{4}$	$\frac{3}{5}$	$\frac{4}{6}$	$\frac{4}{8}$

To prep: If desired, copy onto card stock and laminate for durability. Cut off these directions before copying.

Fractions and Whole Numbers

 Essential Question

How can whole numbers be expressed as fractions?

 Warm-Up/Review

Play Around the World with a set of fraction flash cards.

 Mini-Lesson

1. Draw a triangle on the board. Shade in the whole triangle. Explain, when you divide a shape into 1 equal part, and you shade it all, you have 1 whole.

2. Say, "We can represent this whole by writing 1/1 or saying '1 out of 1.' But, you don't usually hear people say that, you just say 1 whole."

3. Draw 2 more triangles on the board and shade them both in. Ask, "How many wholes do I have now? (3) How can I write these wholes as a fraction?" (3/1) Explain that the numerator of 3 is describing the 3 parts that are shaded and the denominator of 1 is describing the fact that each whole was not divided, so it has only 1 part.

4. Demonstrate how to divide other shapes into equal parts and shade in all equal parts. Explain that when you have all parts of a divided shape shaded, the numerator and denominator are the same number (for example, 5/5), which equals 1 whole.

5. Have students practice showing whole numbers as fractions with other numbers, such as fourths, fifths, and sixths.

6. Challenge students to figure out how 12/3 and 4/1 are related. Have volunteers draw a model for each fraction and discuss.

 Math Talk

When would you need to describe whole numbers as fractions?
Is 3/3 equivalent to 5/5? Why or why not?
Explain the difference between the fractions 4/1 and 4/4. Use pictures and words to help you.

 Journal Prompt

Draw 3 fraction models, each showing 4 wholes. Use a different denominator for each fraction model.

Materials

fraction tiles (or cut-apart fraction bars)
blank laminated number lines
dry-erase markers

 Workstations

Activity sheets (pages 101–103)
Fraction Dominoes (page 104)

 Guided Math

○ **Remediation: Using Fraction Models**

1. Give each student a fraction tile representing 1 whole. Model how 2 halves (1/2 and 1/2) are equivalent to 1 whole by putting the halves on top of the whole. Ask, "How would you write this whole as a fraction?" (2/2)

2. Give each student the thirds fraction tiles. Have them demonstrate how to show how many thirds equal 1 whole. They should show how 3 thirds fit on top of, or line up with 1 whole. Ask what the related fraction would be. (3/3)

3. Continue practicing with the other fraction tiles to show how many of each fraction tile equal 1 whole. Have students practice writing each related fraction as well.

☐ **On Level: Fractions as Whole Numbers**

1. Have students label a laminated blank number line with *0* to *5* on top. Say, "On the bottom of this whole number line we are going to label these whole numbers as fractions. So, under 0 we label it *0/1* because we jump 0 places on the whole number line. Under 1 we label it *1/1* because we jump 1 space on the whole number line. Under 2 we label it *2/1* because we jump 2 spaces on the whole number line." Have students finish labeling the number line.

2. Erase the number line and re-mark it as described at the beginning of step 1. Explain that this number line represents halves. Add a mark between each whole number. Work together to label the whole numbers as fractions. Explain that under 1, we jumped 2 spaces on the number line, so we write 2/2. Be sure students understand that the denominator this time is 2 because this number line is representing halves, whereas the previous number line was representing wholes (1). Work together to finish the number line (4/2, 6/2, 8/2, 10/2).

3. Practice with other number lines, such as thirds, fourths, and fifths.

△ **Enrichment: Improper Fractions and Mixed Numbers**

1. Draw 3 circles, each divided into fifths with all parts shaded. Have students write the fraction and whole number below each circle. (5/5, 1) Say, "If we were to add all of the pieces of the circles together, how many pieces would we have? (15) How would we write that as a fraction? (15/5) When the numerator of a fraction is larger than the denominator, that is called an *improper fraction*."

2. Draw 3 new circles, each divided into thirds. Shade all parts of the first 2 circles, but only shade 1 part of the third circle. Have students write the fractions below each circle (3/3, 3/3, 1/3). Say, "This time, if we add all of the pieces of the circles together, how many pieces would we have? (7) What would that look like as a fraction? (7/3)"

3. Explain that another way to show an improper fraction would be to count how many wholes there are (2) and write the fraction of the whole that is left over (1/3). Therefore, 2 and 1/3 is the same as 7/3. It is called a *mixed number* because it uses both whole numbers and fractions.

4. Continue practicing with other improper fractions and mixed numbers.

 Assess and Extend

Have students solve the following problem: *Felicia baked 3 sheet cakes for a party. She divided the cakes into eighths. Write a fraction that shows the amount of cake Felicia baked for the party. When Felicia arrives at the party she finds that someone else baked 3 more sheet cakes divided into eighths.* How should the fraction change to show the total amount of cake at the party? Draw a picture to show your work.

$\frac{1}{4}$ **Fractions and Whole Numbers**   ● Using Fraction Models

Write the shaded portions of each shape as a fraction.

1. 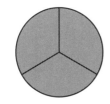 $\dfrac{\square}{\square}$

2.  $\dfrac{\square}{\square}$

3. 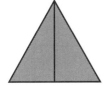 $\dfrac{\square}{\square}$

4. 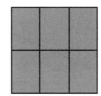 $\dfrac{\square}{\square}$

Write the whole number each fraction is equal to.

5. $\dfrac{5}{5}$ _____

6. $\dfrac{4}{4}$ _____

7. $\dfrac{7}{7}$ _____

8. $\dfrac{12}{12}$ _____

Shade each shape to create a whole.

9.

10.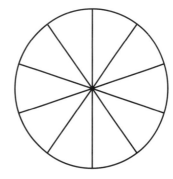

$\frac{1}{4}$ **Fractions and Whole Numbers** ■ Fractions as Whole Numbers

Divide each number line and label it with the appropriate fractions.

1. halves

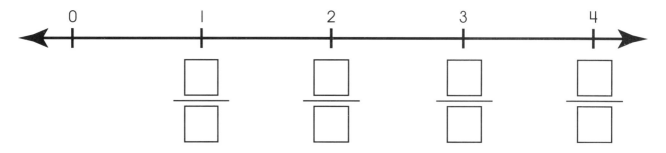

2. fourths

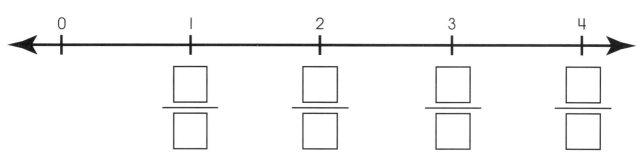

3. sixths

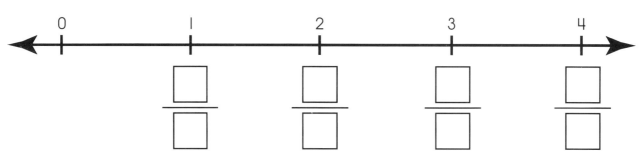

4. eighths

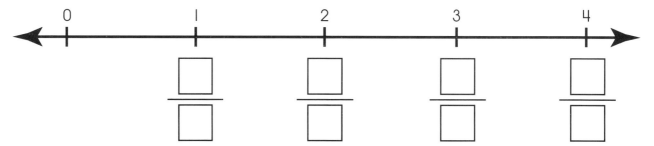

¼ Fractions and Whole Numbers   ▲ Improper Fractions and Mixed Numbers

Draw a model to show each improper fraction. Then, write the mixed number.

1. $\frac{13}{4}$ =

2. $\frac{10}{4}$ =

3. $\frac{18}{8}$ =

4. $\frac{21}{5}$ =

5. $\frac{15}{7}$ =

6. $\frac{23}{6}$ =

7. $\frac{7}{3}$ =

8. $\frac{19}{6}$ =

9. $\frac{17}{9}$ =

10. $\frac{9}{2}$ =

11. $\frac{39}{4}$ =

12. $\frac{15}{6}$ =

Fraction Dominoes

Materials: dominoes, laminated blank number lines, dry-erase markers, scrap paper

Directions: Each player chooses a domino. Place it vertically so that the higher number is on top (numerator) to create an improper fraction. Draw a model to show your improper fraction, then write it as a mixed number (see example below).

Challenge: Each player chooses a domino. Place it vertically so that the higher number is on top (numerator) to create an improper fraction. Using a laminated blank number line, partition your number line and label the sections to show where you would find this improper fraction.

Examples

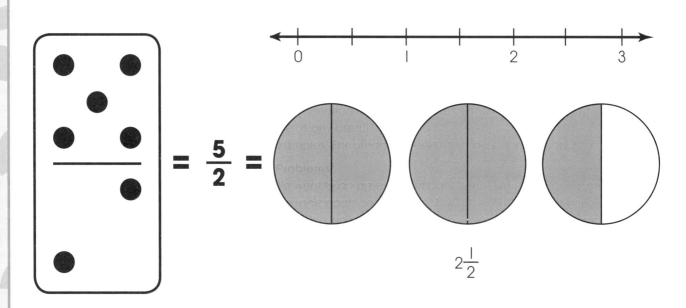

$$= \frac{5}{2} =$$

$$2\frac{1}{2}$$

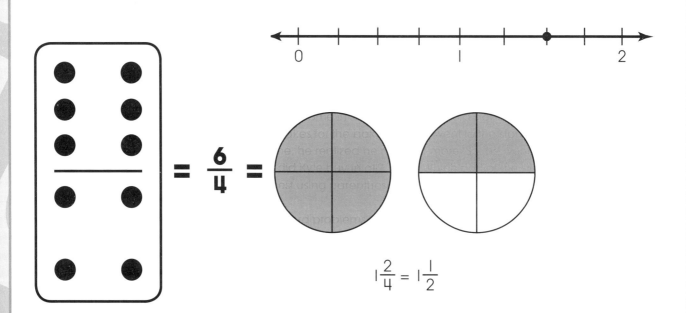

$$= \frac{6}{4} =$$

$$1\frac{2}{4} = 1\frac{1}{2}$$

Essential Question

How can fractions be compared?

 Warm-Up/Review

Give each student a fraction flash card and have her write or model an equivalent fraction. Then, switch cards and repeat as time allows.

 Mini-Lesson

1. Write the fractions *1/8* and *1/2* on the board. Say, "We are going to compare one-eighth and one-half and decide which one is larger."

2. Explain that if the numerators in 2 fractions are the same, you look at the denominators, because they both show 1 part of the whole. The fraction with the smaller denominator is divided into fewer, larger pieces, so it is the greater fraction.

3. Draw models for the fractions to compare the sizes of the pieces. Ask, "Are the numerators the same? (Yes) Which fraction has the smaller denominator? (1/2) So, which fraction is greater? (1/2)"

4. Write the fractions *1/4* and *3/4* on the board. Say, "We can also compare fractions that have the same denominator." Explain that if the denominators are the same, you compare the numerators because the wholes are divided into the same size and number of pieces. The fraction with the bigger numerator has more of the same-size pieces, so it is greater.

5. Draw models for the fractions to compare the number of pieces. Ask, "Are the denominators the same? (Yes) Which fraction has the bigger numerator? (3/4) So, which fraction is greater? (3/4)"

6. Continue comparing and modeling other fraction pairs that have the same numerator or denominator.

 Math Talk

What's the first thing you do when comparing fractions?
Tell another strategy you can use when comparing fractions.
Do you think it is possible to compare fractions with different denominators and numerators? Why or why not?

 Journal Prompt

Draw a circle divided into sixths with 4 parts shaded, and a circle divided into eighths with 8 parts shaded. How do these two fractions compare to each other? Explain your answer using words and numbers.

Materials

fraction tiles (or cut-apart fraction bars)
chart paper

 Workstations

Activity sheets (pages 107–109)
Comparing Fractions Bump
(page 110)

 Guided Math

○ Remediation: Using Models

1. Write the fractions *1/4* and *1/3*. Have students choose a 1/4 and 1/3 fraction tile. Tell students to line the fraction tiles up one above the other. Ask, "Which fraction tile is larger?" (1/3)

2. Write the fractions *3/5* and *3/8*. Again, have students choose three 1/5 fraction tiles and three 1/8 fraction tiles. Tell them to line the fraction tiles up one above the other. Ask, "Which group of fraction tiles is larger?" (3/5)

3. Remind students of the mini-lesson in which they learned that if the numerators are the same, the fraction with the smaller denominator will always be the larger fraction, which was true for both examples they saw in this lesson. A smaller denominator means that there are fewer, larger pieces.

4. Continue to have students practice comparing additional fraction pairs with different denominators or different numerators.

☐ On Level: Prove It

1. Write *1/4 < 1/3*. Ask, "Is this comparison true or false? How do you know?" Students should come to the conclusion that 1/3 is greater than 1/4 because both fractions share the same numerator, therefore the fraction with the smaller denominator is the greater fraction.

2. Write *2/5 > 4/5*. Have students determine if this comparison is true or false. Have students explain using words or pictures why this comparison is false and how it should be shown correctly. Students should come to the conclusion that this statement is false because 2/5 and 4/5 share the same denominator, therefore the fraction with the greater numerator (4/5) is the greater fraction.

3. Continue practicing with fraction pairs with the same numerators or the same denominators. Have students prove their comparison each time using words or pictures.

△ Enrichment: Using Benchmark Fractions

1. Write the fractions *1/6* and *2/3*. Explain that students can easily compare fractions with unlike denominators by using benchmark fractions.

2. First, review benchmark fractions and be sure all students are familiar with common benchmark fractions, such as 1/4, 1/3, 1/2, 2/3, and 3/4. Create a chart with visuals of benchmark fractions for students to refer back to.

3. Explain that you know 1/6 is less than 3/6, and 3/6 is equal to 1/2, so 1/6 is less than 1/2. You know that 2/3 is greater than 1/2, therefore 1/6 < 2/3.

4. Have students practice with other fraction pairs with unlike denominators. Encourage students to explain their thinking using benchmark fractions to justify each comparison.

 Assess and Extend

Ask students to explain how to compare the fractions 3/8 and 3/10 using words and/or models.

¼ Comparing Fractions   ● Using Models

Write a fraction for the shaded area of each figure. Then, write >, <, or = to compare each pair of fractions.

1.

___ ◯ ___

2.

___ ◯ ___

3.

___ ◯ ___

4.

___ ◯ ___

5.

___ ◯ ___

6.

___ ◯ ___

7.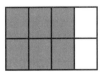

___ ◯ ___

8.

___ ◯ ___

$\frac{1}{4}$ Comparing Fractions   ☐ Prove It

Circle the comparisons in each set that are not true. Rewrite the false comparisons so that they are true. Draw pictures to prove your corrections.

1. $\frac{1}{4} < \frac{1}{3}$ $\frac{1}{6} > \frac{1}{9}$ $\frac{1}{5} > \frac{1}{2}$ $\frac{1}{6} > \frac{1}{3}$ $\frac{1}{7} > \frac{1}{10}$

2. $\frac{2}{5} > \frac{4}{5}$ $\frac{2}{10} < \frac{8}{10}$ $\frac{1}{3} < \frac{2}{3}$ $\frac{4}{8} > \frac{6}{8}$ $\frac{1}{9} < \frac{4}{9}$

3. $\frac{1}{2} < \frac{1}{4}$ $\frac{3}{4} > \frac{1}{4}$ $\frac{5}{6} < \frac{2}{6}$ $\frac{5}{6} < \frac{5}{12}$ $\frac{4}{5} > \frac{2}{5}$

4. $\frac{5}{8} > \frac{2}{8}$ $\frac{2}{9} > \frac{3}{9}$ $\frac{2}{9} > \frac{4}{9}$ $\frac{1}{7} > \frac{1}{12}$ $\frac{1}{2} > \frac{1}{11}$

5. $\frac{4}{5} > \frac{3}{5}$ $\frac{2}{6} < \frac{5}{6}$ $\frac{1}{3} < \frac{1}{6}$ $\frac{3}{7} > \frac{1}{7}$ $\frac{1}{5} > \frac{1}{8}$

6. $\frac{1}{7} > \frac{1}{8}$ $\frac{1}{5} > \frac{1}{3}$ $\frac{7}{9} > \frac{3}{9}$ $\frac{4}{10} < \frac{7}{10}$ $\frac{5}{6} < \frac{3}{6}$

¼ Comparing Fractions   ▲ Using Benchmark Fractions

Write >, <, or = to compare each pair of fractions.

1. $\frac{5}{10}$ ◯ $\frac{2}{5}$

2. $\frac{1}{6}$ ◯ $\frac{2}{3}$

3. $\frac{1}{14}$ ◯ $\frac{6}{7}$

4. $\frac{5}{10}$ ◯ $\frac{2}{3}$

5. $\frac{1}{12}$ ◯ $\frac{3}{8}$

6. $\frac{6}{7}$ ◯ $\frac{3}{21}$

7. $\frac{4}{7}$ ◯ $\frac{8}{14}$

8. $\frac{3}{5}$ ◯ $\frac{1}{2}$

9. $\frac{4}{6}$ ◯ $\frac{7}{8}$

10. $\frac{1}{7}$ ◯ $\frac{4}{21}$

11. $\frac{3}{8}$ ◯ $\frac{1}{2}$

12. $\frac{2}{3}$ ◯ $\frac{7}{9}$

13. $\frac{6}{7}$ ◯ $\frac{1}{3}$

14. $\frac{1}{6}$ ◯ $\frac{2}{12}$

15. $\frac{3}{5}$ ◯ $\frac{1}{15}$

16. $\frac{4}{5}$ ◯ $\frac{1}{4}$

17. $\frac{5}{8}$ ◯ $\frac{15}{24}$

18. $\frac{1}{3}$ ◯ $\frac{4}{9}$

Comparing Fractions Bump

Materials: 2 dice, 10 two-color counters per player

To play: Players take turns. Place a counter on Start for each player. Roll the dice and move that many spaces. Compare the fraction you landed on to a fraction in the center of the board. Player 2 confirms whether player 1 has compared the fractions correctly. If correct, player 1 can cover up the fraction in the center of the board. If incorrect, player 2 takes a turn. You can "bump" the other player off of a space if they have only 1 counter on it. Once you place 2 counters on a space, it is yours and cannot be bumped. The first player to use all of his counters wins.

Start →	$\frac{3}{4}$	$\frac{1}{3}$	$\frac{2}{5}$	$\frac{1}{2}$	$\frac{2}{8}$
$\frac{8}{10}$					$\frac{8}{8}$
$\frac{4}{8}$					$\frac{2}{10}$
$\frac{2}{10}$					$\frac{1}{3}$
$\frac{5}{8}$					$\frac{4}{8}$
$\frac{2}{5}$	$\frac{2}{3}$	$\frac{3}{4}$	$\frac{3}{5}$	$\frac{4}{6}$	$\frac{8}{10}$

- ✂

To prep: If desired, copy onto card stock and laminate for durability. Cut off these directions before copying.

Time to the Minute

 ## Essential Question

How can time be expressed to the nearest minute?

 ## Warm-Up/Review

Review the hands of a clock. Ask, "How many minutes does each number represent on the clock?" Students should remember that every number represents 5 minutes on the clock. Show 2:15 on a clock with movable hands. Have students tell you the time.

 ## Mini-Lesson

Materials: 1 clock with movable hands for each student, larger clock with movable hands for teacher

1. Give each student a clock with movable hands. Have them look for the marks on the clock in between each number.

2. Say, "We know that each number on a clock represents 5 minutes. The marks in between each number represent 1 minute." It may be helpful to explain how this is similar to a number line in the sense that the space in between numbers is divided into smaller amounts that count up by 1s.

3. Write *6:19* on the board. Have students model the time on a clock with movable hands. Check and repeat with several more times.

4. Say, "A third grader arrives at school at 8:10. Four minutes later, she starts her morning work. What time does the third grader start her morning work?" Model on the clock where 8:10 is, then move the minute hand ahead 4 minutes and count to 8:14.

5. Continue practicing with other time problems where students must practice finding time to the nearest minute.

 ## Math Talk

What is the first step you should do when finding the time?

Is there another way to solve these problems without using the clocks? Explain.

Why is it important to know how to tell time to the nearest minute?

 ## Journal Prompt

Record the times you wake up, leave for school, arrive home, do your homework, and go to sleep. Draw each time on a clock using the correct placement of the hour and minute hands.

Materials

large clock with movable hands
small clocks with movable hands
laminated blank clocks
dry-erase markers

 Workstations

Activity sheets (pages 113–115)
Rock Around the Clock (page 116)

 Guided Math

○ **Remediation: Practicing with a Clock**

1. Show the time 1:22 on a clock with movable hands. Ask, "What time does this clock show?"

2. Explain that the hour hand (short hand) is just past the 1, which tells us that it is past 1 o'clock but not yet 2 o'clock. The minute hand (long hand) tells us it is 22 minutes past 1 because it is on the second mark after the 4. (If students struggle with this concept, it may be helpful to revisit the number line analogy from the mini-lesson or skip count by 5s and 1s while pointing to the numbers and tick marks.) Have students practice reading more times from the large clock and explaining their thought process.

3. Write *3:57*. Give each student a clock with movable hands. Say, "Show me 3:57 on your clock."

4. Model how to put the hour hand (short hand) past the 3 on the clock, and the minute hand (long hand) on the second mark after 11. Continue to have students practice showing more times on their clocks with movable hands.

☐ **On Level: Drawing Hands on a Clock**

1. Write *3:48*. Give each student a laminated blank clock. Have them draw the hands on the clock to show the time 3:48.

2. Demonstrate how the hour hand (the short hand) should be more than halfway past the 3 because it is after 3:30 and closer to 4:00. Demonstrate how the minute hand (long hand) should be on the third mark past the 9 because the 9 represents 45 minutes, and 3 marks past 45 is 48 minutes.

3. Write more times, such as *2:14*, *5:27*, *8:11*, and *11:56*. Have students draw hands on the clock showing each time.

4. Have students draw times on a laminated clock. Have them trade clocks with a partner and read and write the time shown.

△ **Enrichment: Using Time Vocabulary**

1. Draw a clock and add a line going through the 12 down through the 6. Then, draw a line going through the 9 over through the 3. Say, "I have just divided this clock into four equal parts, or *quarters.*"

2. Explain that when the minute hand is on the 3, you can say it is "quarter past" the hour you are in. Show them a clock with movable hands at 4:15 and say, "It is quarter past 4." Explain that when the minute hand is on the 6, you can say it is "half past" the hour you are in. Move the minute hand to 6 and say, "It is half past 4." Explain that when the minute hand is on the 9, you can say it is "quarter till" the next hour. Move the minute hand to the 9 and say, "It is quarter till 5."

3. Give each student a laminated blank clock. Say, "Draw the hands to show quarter till 7." Discuss how the hour hand should be drawn more than halfway past the 6 because it is after 6:30 and closer to 7:00.

4. Have students continue practicing with more times as you call them out.

 Assess and Extend

Give each student a sticky note to put on the corner of their desk. Throughout the day, call out the phrase, "time check." Students should look at the main analog clock in the classroom and write down the exact time. Keep track of what times you called "time check" and collect all the sticky notes at the end of the day. Check students' times with your times to see who may need more assistance.

Time to the Minute

Write the time shown on each clock.

1.

_____

2.

_____

3.

_____

4.

_____

5.

_____

6.

_____

7.

_____

8.

_____

9.

_____

10.

_____

11.

_____

12.

_____

13.

_____

14.

_____

15.

_____

16.

_____

Time to the Minute   ☐ **Drawing Hands on a Clock**

Draw the hands on the clock face for the time shown.

1.	**2.**	**3.**	**4.**
8:04	5:26	4:11	7:25
5.	**6.**	**7.**	**8.**
6:57	10:01	12:38	3:17
9.	**10.**	**11.**	**12.**
11:09	2:41	1:52	12:07
13.	**14.**	**15.**	**16.**
12:55	4:19	9:31	10:10

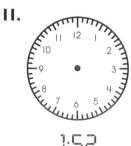
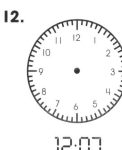

Name _____   Date _____

 Time to the Minute   ▲ Using Time Vocabulary

Draw the hands on the clock face for the time shown.

I.
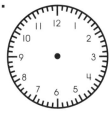
half past nine

2.

quarter till five

3.

half past ten

4.

quarter
after one

5.

quarter after
three

6.
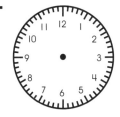
half past eleven

7.

quarter till twelve

8.

quarter
after six

9.
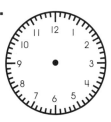
half past eight

10.

half past two

II.

quarter after seven

12.

quarter
till nine

13.
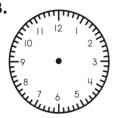
half past seven

14.

quarter after ten

15.
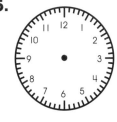
quarter till eight

16.

half past
twelve

Rock Around the Clock

Materials: 1 die, 1 two-color counter per player, 2 different color crayons

To play: Players take turns. Roll the die and move that many spaces clockwise around the clock. Player 1 says the time she landed on and finds the analog clock inside the circle that matches. Player 2 checks the time. If Player 1 is correct, she colors the analog clock. If not, the next player takes a turn. The player with the most clocks colored at the end of the game wins.

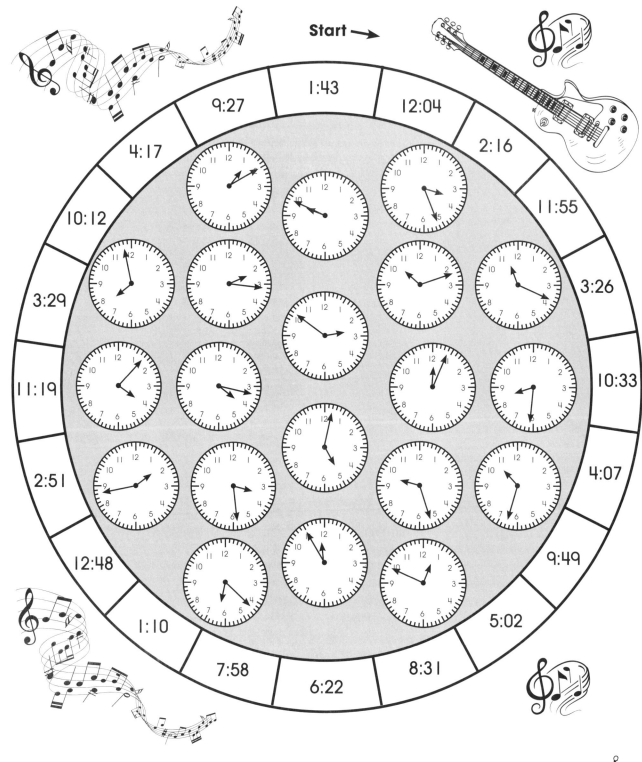

- ✂

To prep: If desired, copy onto card stock and laminate for durability. Cut off these directions before copying.

Elapsed Time

 Essential Question

What strategies can help solve time problems?

 Warm-Up/Review

Review telling time to the minute by having students demonstrate where the hands on a clock with movable hands should go to show the times 4:34, 11:21, 6:58, 2:10, and 9:04.

 Mini-Lesson

Materials: clock with movable hands

1. Explain that there are two methods that can be used to determine elapsed time. The first method is counting on a clock. Read the following problem: *The basketball game started at 6:00. It lasted 2 hours and 3 minutes. What time did it end?*

2. Say, "First, start at 6:00. Show 6:00 on your clocks. Next, add or count the full hours." Model how to count 2 hours and move the hour hand to the 8. Say, "Now, add or count the minutes." Model how to count 3 minutes and move the minute hand to the third mark past the 12. Have students read the time on the clock. (8:03)

3. The second method is drawing a number line. Explain and model for students how to draw a line and mark the start time (6:00). Mark off the time from the starting hour to each of the next 2 hours (8:00), writing the amount of elapsed time by each mark. Then, mark off and label the 3 minutes. Add the labeled amounts to find the total elapsed time. (2 hr. 3 min.)

4. Continue practicing with more elapsed time problems, using both a clock and a number line. Be sure to include problems where students add hours to a given time and problems where they determine how much time has passed between two given times.

 Math Talk

Are there other ways to determine elapsed time? Explain.

What did you need to know to answer these questions?

How can we use elapsed time in our daily lives?

 Journal Prompt

Write a definition of elapsed *time* in your own words.

Materials

clock with movable hands

 Workstations

Activity sheets (pages 119–121)
Elapsed Time Four-in-a-Row
   (page 122)
Rock Around the Clock (page 116)

 Guided Math

○ **Remediation: Simple Elapsed Time**

1. Share the following problem: *It began to rain at 2:00. It stopped raining at 5:00. How long did it rain?* Explain that we can use a clock with movable hands to show how much time has passed (elapsed).

2. Demonstrate how to start with the given time, 2:00. Then, show how to move the hour hand from 2 to 5, counting how many hours have passed.

3. Say, "Three hours have passed between 2:00 and 5:00, therefore it rained for 3 hours."

4. Continue practicing with more simple elapsed time problems.

☐ **On Level: Using a T-Chart**

1. Share the following problem: *The sun came out at 6:39. It set at 4:47. How long was the sun out?* Explain that we can use a T-chart to figure out how much time has gone by.

2. Have students write 6:39 and 4:47 at the top of a T-chart. Ask, "Beginning with 6:39, how many hours can we count on to get us close to 4:47?" Model for students how to count ahead 10 hours. "So, in 10 hours it will be 4:39. In our T-chart under 6:39 let's write *4:39*. Since we counted 10 hours, write on the other side of the T-chart *10 hours*. We cannot count another hour because we will go over, so let's count minutes. I'm going to start with 5 minutes, because 10 minutes would be too many minutes and 5 is easy. So, add 5 minutes to 4:39 and we get 4:44. Write *4:44* under 4:39 in the T-chart. Then, write *5 minutes* on the other side. Finally, how many minutes do we need to get to our end time of 4:47? Three minutes. Write *4:47* under 4:44, and write *3 minutes* on the other side of the T-chart."

3. Explain that next, you add up the time amounts on the right side of the chart to find the elapsed time. (10 hours + 5 minutes + 3 minutes = 10 hours and 8 minutes). Therefore, the sun was out for 10 hours and 8 minutes.

4. Continue to practice with more elapsed time problems, having students use a T-chart.

△ **Enrichment: Elapsed Time Word Problems**

1. Write the time *6:30*, as well as *53 minutes*.

2. Ask students to write an elapsed time problem that would make sense with this start time, and the amount of time that has gone by. "Say you can use am or pm. What kinds of activities might begin at 6:30 am or pm and last for 53 minutes?" Write the example, *Jeremy woke up at 6:30. He takes a shower, brushes his teeth and hair, gets dressed, and has breakfast. All of this takes him 53 minutes. At what time is Jeremy ready to go to school?*

3. Direct students to write their own word problems for the same instance of elapsed time. Discuss students' stories. Have students trade stories with a partner and have the partner solve.

4. Continue writing word problems for other instances of elapsed times.

 Assess and Extend

Have students solve the following problems: *Hector leaves for work at 8:07 am. He drives for 21 minutes.* What time does he get to work? (8:28) *Hector has 1 hour for lunch. He leaves work at 12:05 and drives for 12 minutes to get to where he is going to eat lunch. He spends 35 minutes eating lunch. Then, he drives for 12 minutes back to work.* At what time does Hector get back to work? (1:04)

Name _____ Date _____

Find each amount of time that has passed. Use the clocks for help.

1. The sun came out at 5:00. It set at 4:00. How long was the sun out?

_____ hours

2. It began to rain at 4:00. It stopped raining at 8:00. How long did it rain?

_____ hours

3. A rainbow appeared at 6:00. It disappeared at 8:00. How long did the rainbow last?

_____ hours

4. The wind started blowing at 11:00. It stopped at 4:00. How long did the wind blow?

_____ hours

5. Brad starting riding his bike at 3:00. He stopped and came home at 5:00. How long did Brad ride his bike?

_____ hours

6. Ellen's favorite movie starts at 7:00. The movie is over at 10:00. How long is Ellen's favorite movie?

_____ hours

Elapsed Time   ■ **Using a T-Chart**

Read each problem. Use clocks or number lines to solve.

1. It is 12:03. The class will return from the library at 12:35. How many minutes until the class returns?

_____

2. It is 7:11. The movie starts at 8:30. How long until the movie starts?

_____

3. It is 4:43. Dinner is at 5:15. How long until dinner?

_____

4. The pie takes 52 minutes to bake. I put it in the oven at 6:12. When will it be done?

_____

5. The gym is 19 minutes away. If we leave at 4:10, when do we arrive at the gym?

_____

6. Jack's new game shuts down after 45 minutes. He started the game at 4:48. When will the game turn itself off?

_____

7. Room 12 goes to music at 2:35. Music is done at 3:15. How long is music?

_____

8. The show is 48 minutes long. It starts at 8:07. What time will the show be over?

_____

9. It is 10:18. The train comes at 10:34. How long until the train comes?

_____

10. Sheila ran 2 miles in 16 minutes. She started at 2:49. When did she finish?

_____

Elapsed Time   ▲ Elapsed Time Word Problems

Write a word problem to describe each instance of elapsed time.

1. 4:05; 3 hours 13 minutes

_____

_____

_____

_____

2. 8:03; 8 hours 9 minutes

_____

_____

_____

_____

3. 10:07; 7 hours 42 minutes

_____

_____

_____

_____

4. 6:05; 37 minutes

_____

_____

_____

_____

5. 7:55; 1 hour 33 minutes

_____

_____

_____

_____

Elapsed Time Four-in-a-Row

Materials: I die, I different colored pencil for each player

To play: Players take turns. Each player rolls the die once to determine what time an activity starts and once to determine what time an activity ends. Once the player finds the elapsed time, he marks off one side of a square showing the elapsed time in minutes. The player to draw the last border on a square colors it in. If there is not a blank square showing the correct elapsed time, the player loses her turn. The player that colors the most squares wins.

Die Face	Roll #1 – Start Time	Roll #2 – End Time
(1)	2:35	3:14
(2)	2:18	2:56
(3)	2:15	3:00
(4)	2:27	3:12
(5)	2:41	3:02
(6)	2:14	2:45

```
•   •   •   •   •   •   •   •   •   •
  39  31  39  21  33  18  42  37  42  30
•   •   •   •   •   •   •   •   •   •
  54  15  37  42  38  60  44   4  10  54
•   •   •   •   •   •   •   •   •   •
  41  31  58  35  30  45  31  45  47  46
•   •   •   •   •   •   •   •   •   •
  30  47  59  47  57  27  60  33  48  33
•   •   •   •   •   •   •   •   •   •
  31  21  19  27  57  19  48  25  58  59
•   •   •   •   •   •   •   •   •   •
  56  44  27  21  56  33  46  27  37  25
•   •   •   •   •   •   •   •   •   •
  21  27  29  35  19  25  42  45  10  54
•   •   •   •   •   •   •   •   •   •
  15   4  18  41  47   4  30  29  38  33
•   •   •   •   •   •   •   •   •   •
```

Measuring Mass

 Warm-Up/Review

Review the word *mass*. Ask students, "What does the statement, 'The mass of the tennis ball is 10 grams,' tell us about the word *mass*?" Ask, "Are there any other units for measuring mass?"

 Mini-Lesson

Materials: paper clips, 2-pound bag of rice

1. Distribute a paper clip to each student and tell them to hold it in the palm of their hand. Explain that 1 paper clip weighs about 1 gram. Say, "We use the unit *gram* to describe the masses of lighter objects, such as a paper clip."

2. Show students a 2-pound bag of rice. Allow students to hold the bag of rice and feel the weight of it. Explain that this bag of rice weighs about 1 kilogram. Say, "We use the unit *kilogram* to describe the masses of heavier objects, such as a bag of rice."

3. Draw a T-chart on the board. Write *grams* and *kilograms* on either side. Have students identify objects around the room that would be measured using grams or kilograms and add them in the appropriate column on the T-chart. (Answers will vary but may include: *grams—pencil, piece of paper, folder; kilograms—desk, chair, table, bookshelf.*)

4. Continue to have students share, and allow them to hold and feel the mass of certain objects if they are unsure.

 Math Talk

Are there other words that are used to describe the mass of something? What words?

Why do you think there are different words for describing mass?

Why might it be important to know an object's mass?

 Journal Prompt

Make a T-chart of various items that you would find outside that would have a mass in grams or kilograms.

Materials

various lightweight objects
various heavier objects
balance scale with weights

 Workstations

Activity sheets (pages 125–127)
Mass Comparison Task Cards
(page 128)

 Guided Math

⚪ **Remediation: Hands-On Mass**

1. Show students various objects that would be measured in grams and kilograms, such as a balloon, pencil, eraser, ball, a large hardcover book, a chair, a brick, a large bag of flour, etc.
2. Allow students to touch, hold, and pick up each object to feel its mass. Have students work together to sort the objects into 2 groups: objects measured in grams, and objects measured in kilograms. Discuss why each object would be measured in either unit.
3. Next, have students go on a scavenger hunt around the room. Have them write down objects they think would be measured using grams, and objects they would measure using kilograms.
4. Continue practicing with tangible objects. If possible, take students to different places to complete their scavenger hunt, such as outside or the library.

⬜ **On Level: Mass Word Problems**

1. Show students the following problem: *Hunter has 33 grams of cheese. Pilar has 65 grams of cheese. How many grams of cheese do Hunter and Pilar have altogether?*
2. Ask, "What is this problem asking me to do?" Students should say it wants them to add together Hunter and Pilar's amounts of cheese because the problem uses the word *altogether*.
3. Write *33 grams + 65 grams =* vertically. Have students solve. Students should determine that altogether, Hunter and Pilar have 98 grams of cheese.
4. Explain that with measurement word problems, it is important to label your answer with the appropriate units, which in this case is grams.
5. Practice with another problem, such as: *Patrick weighed 4 kilograms when he was born. On his second birthday, he weighed 15 kilograms. How much weight did Patrick gain since his birth?* (11 kg)

🔺 **Enrichment: Measuring Mass**

1. Demonstrate how to use a balance scale by placing an object with an unknown mass in one bucket of the balance scale and adding weights to the other bucket to balance the scale.
2. Explain that to find the mass of an unknown object, they must balance the scale so that it is even on both sides. Explain how students can also make *greater than/less than* statements, such as "The glue stick is greater than 10 grams, but less than 100 grams." or "The glue stick has less mass than the book."
3. Allow students to continue measuring objects of different masses. Have them record their findings and make *greater than* or *less than* statements.

 Assess and Extend

Have students solve the following problem: *A saltshaker holds 6 grams of salt. If there are 30 saltshakers in the restaurant, how many grams of salt are in the restaurant?* (180 g)

Measuring Mass ⬤ Hands-On Mass

Circle the correct unit to measure each item.

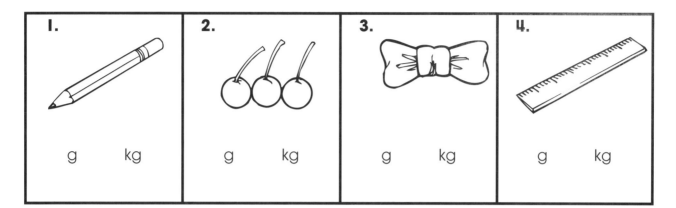

1. g kg

2. g kg

3. g kg

4. g kg

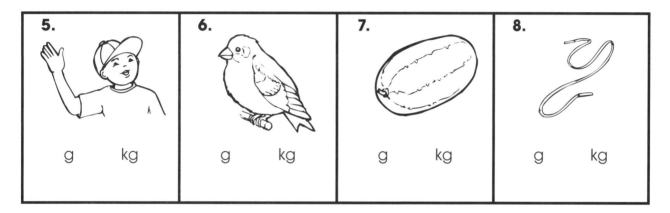

5. g kg

6. g kg

7. g kg

8. g kg

Solve.

9. A party hat has a mass of 20 grams. What is the total mass of a set of 5 party hats?

10. A bag of buttons has a mass of 54 grams. Norman wants to divide the buttons evenly into 6 smaller bags. What will be the mass of each smaller bag of buttons?

Measuring Mass   ☐ Mass Word Problems

Solve.

1. Orlando packed 18 kilograms of apples equally into 3 bags. How many kilograms of apples are in each bag?

2. An adult weighs about 65 kilograms. An adult male black bear weighs 389 kilograms. How much more does a black bear weigh than a human?

3. Monica, Simone, and Whitney each have a book bag that weighs 5 kilograms. How many kilograms do their book bags weigh in all?

4. Samantha has a collection of bouncy balls. Each ball weighs 7 grams. Her whole collection weighs 420 grams. How many bouncy balls are in Samantha's collection?

5. Spencer has 9 plants around his house. Each plant weighs 6 kilograms. How many kilograms do the plants weigh altogether?

6. Reba checks out two books from the library. The fiction book she checks out weighs 321 grams. The nonfiction book she checks out weighs 419 grams. What is the total mass of Reba's two library books?

7. Victor and Tristan grow pumpkins in their backyards. Victor's pumpkin grows to a mass of 795 grams. Tristan's pumpkin grows to a mass of 843 grams. How much heavier is Tristan's pumpkin than Victor's?

Measuring Mass ▲ Measuring Mass

Write the best unit to measure each item (g or kg).

1. a bus _____

2. a brownie _____

3. a crayon _____

4. a bookshelf _____

5. a book _____

6. a four-wheeler _____

7. a pair of socks _____

8. a bathtub _____

Solve.

9. Gregory took all his laundry to the laundry mat. They measured the mass of his clothes to determine the cost of his laundry. Gregory's laundry measured 50 kilograms. If it costs $8 per kilogram of laundry, how much will Gregory have to pay to have his laundry cleaned?

10. Destiny collected eggs on the farm this morning. Each egg weighed 51 grams. If Destiny collected 9 eggs, how many total grams of eggs did Destiny collect?

11. Carson has a male and a female horse. The female horse has a mass of 450 kilograms. The male horse has a mass of 796 kilograms. How much greater is the mass of the male horse than the female horse?

12. A large box contains 10 bags of sugar. If the box has a mass of 500 kilograms, what is the approximate mass of each bag of sugar?

13. Anna and Byron bought some candy at the store. Anna's bag of candy had a mass of 312 grams. Byron's bag of candy had a mass of 433 grams. What is the total mass of Byron and Anna's bags of candy?

Mass Comparison Task Cards

Materials: balance scale, dry-erase marker, penny, dime, quarter, eraser, pencil, colored pencil, marker, pen, crayon, full crayon box, paper, paper clip, scissors, glue stick, glue bottle

To play: Choose a task card. Find the two objects on the task card. Put them on the balance scale. Record the object that has the most mass.

Which has more mass? a pair of scissors your pencil	**Which has more mass?** a crayon a pencil	**Which has more mass?** a glue stick a pair of scissors	**Which has more mass?** a crumpled piece of paper an uncrumpled piece of paper
Which has more mass? a crayon a marker	**Which has more mass?** a glue bottle a box of crayons	**Which has more mass?** a paper clip a piece of paper	**Which has more mass?** a glue stick a marker
Which has more mass? a glue bottle a dry-erase marker	**Which has more mass?** a marker a dry-erase eraser	**Which has more mass?** a dime a quarter	**Which has more mass?** a piece of paper a penny
Which has more mass? a pencil an eraser	**Which has more mass?** a pen a pencil	**Which has more mass?** a glue bottle 2 glue sticks	**Which has more mass?** a colored pencil a regular pencil

To prep: If desired, copy the task cards on card stock and laminate for durability before cutting apart.

Measuring Volume

 Essential Question

How can volume be measured?

 Warm-Up/Review

Review the word *volume*. Ask students, "What does the statement, 'The volume of the water bottle is 16 milliliters,' tell us about the word *volume*?" Ask, "Are there any other units for measuring volume?"

 Mini-Lesson

Materials: bottle of water, 2-liter bottle, picture of a large swimming pool

1. Write the words *milliliters* and *liters* on the board. Tell students that we can measure how much liquid is in something, or how much space an item takes up using the units milliliters and liters. This measurement is called *volume*.

2. Show students a water bottle. Tell them that when measuring a small amount of liquid, we use the unit *milliliters*.

3. Show students a 2-liter bottle. Tell them when measuring a medium amount of liquid, we use the unit *liters*.

4. Show students a picture of a swimming pool. Tell students that if we are measuring how much water is in the swimming pool, we could use a related but larger unit called *kiloliters*.

5. Next, ask students to brainstorm. Have them write down objects they think would be measured using milliliters, liters, and kiloliters in a 3-column T-chart. Discuss students' responses.

 Math Talk

Are there other words that are used to describe the volume of something? What words?
Why do you think there are different words?
Why might it be important to know an object's volume?

 Journal Prompt

Make a collage of photos from magazines showing various objects where you can measure the volume. Label the pictures with *milliliters*, *liters*, or *kiloliters*.

Materials

various pictures of containers that can
be filled with liquid, such as a cup
and milk jug
small containers, such as a cup, water
bottle, spoon, and graduated
cylinders
colored water

 Workstations

Activity sheets (pages 131–133)
Volume Task Cards (page 134)

 Guided Math

◯ **Remediation: Volume Sort**
1. Show students various pictures of containers that can be filled with liquid.
2. Remind students that we use milliliters to measure the volumes of small objects like drinking cups. Say, "We use liters to measure the volumes of medium-sized objects like milk jugs, and we use kiloliters to measure the volumes of large objects like bathtubs."
3. Have students sort the picture cards into 3 groups: milliliters, liters, and kiloliters.
4. Continue to practice by having students brainstorm other containers whose volume would be measured in milliliters, liters, or kiloliters. Have them draw their own pictures and add them to the sort.

▢ **On Level: Volume Word Problems**
1. Show students the following problem: *Before mopping, Mr. Ormond filled a bucket with 8 liters of water. After he mopped one room, he put 6 more liters of water in the bucket. How many liters of water did Mr. Ormond use altogether?*
2. Ask, "What is this problem asking me to do?" Students should say it wants them to add together the amounts of water Mr. Ormond used because the problem uses the word *altogether*.
3. Write *8 liters + 6 liters =* vertically. Have students solve. Students should determine that Mr. Ormond used 14 liters of water altogether.
4. Explain to students that with word problems it is important to label your answer with the appropriate unit, which in this case is liters. Practice with another problem, such as: *Leo drank 23 milliliters of lemonade on Monday. On Tuesday, he drank 42 milliliters of lemonade. How many more milliliters of lemonade did Leo drink on Tuesday?* (19 mL)

△ **Enrichment: Measuring Volume**
1. Demonstrate for students how to find the liquid volume of a container by choosing a container and filling it up with colored water.
2. Carefully pour the colored water into the graduated cylinder. Show students how to carefully read the markings on the side of the graduated cylinder to determine how many milliliters the container can hold.
3. Have students practice in pairs filling up the containers with various amounts of colored water, pouring them into the graduated cylinder, reading the volume, and recording their results.

 Assess and Extend

Have students solve the following problem: *Logan had a fish tank that held 58 liters of water. Logan left the top off the tank, and 7 liters of water evaporated. How many liters of water were left in Logan's fish tank?* (51 L)

130

Name _____ **Date** _____

Measuring Volume

Circle the correct unit to measure each item.

1.  mL　　　L	**2.**  mL　　　L	**3.** 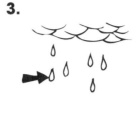 mL　　　L	**4.**  mL　　　L
5. 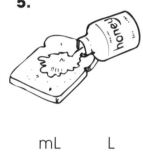 mL　　　L	**6.**  mL　　　L	**7.**  mL　　　L	**8.**  mL　　　L

Solve.

9. Mandy needed to buy juice for her class party. She bought nine 2-liter bottles of juice. How many liters of juice did Mandy buy for the party?

10. Luis boiled 750 mL of water to cook potatoes. He boiled 450 mL of water to cook pasta. How many total milliliters of water did Luis boil to cook both potatoes and pasta?

Name _____ Date _____

Solve.

1. Lamar has a small pool that holds 175 liters of water. He has filled it with 91 liters of water so far. How many more liters can he add to the pool?

2. Matthew's dog's water dish had 350 milliliters of water. His dog drank 112 milliliters; then, his dad added 65 milliliters. How many milliliters of water does the dog's dish have now?

3. Mr. Chadwick bought drinks for a party. Did he buy 13 liters or 14 milliliters of drinks? How do you know?

4. The grocery store stocked 2-liter bottles on the shelves. Each shelf can hold 10 bottles. There are 8 shelves in the section. How many liters can the store display at one time?

5. Penny served herself 308 milliliters of soup. Her sister served herself 298 milliliters of soup. If the pot started with 700 milliliters of soup, is there enough left for Penny's dad to have 300 milliliters? Why or why not?

6. Cara had 400 milliliters of water. Dawson had 245 more milliliters than Cara. How many milliliters of water does Dawson have?

7. Donna made 17 liters of lemonade and 13 liters of iced tea. How many total liters of lemonade and iced tea did she make?

Name _____   Date _____

Write the volume shown on each graduated cylinder. The unit is milliliters.
Hint: Pay attention to the numbers on each graduated cylinder to figure out how much the marks in between are worth.

1.
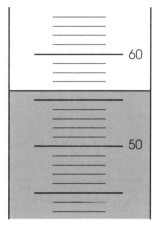

_____

2.
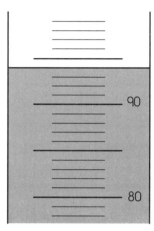

_____

3.

_____

4.

_____

5.
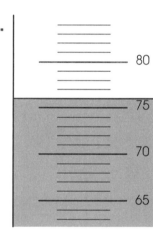

_____

6.

_____

7.

_____

8.

_____

9.

_____

Volume Task Cards

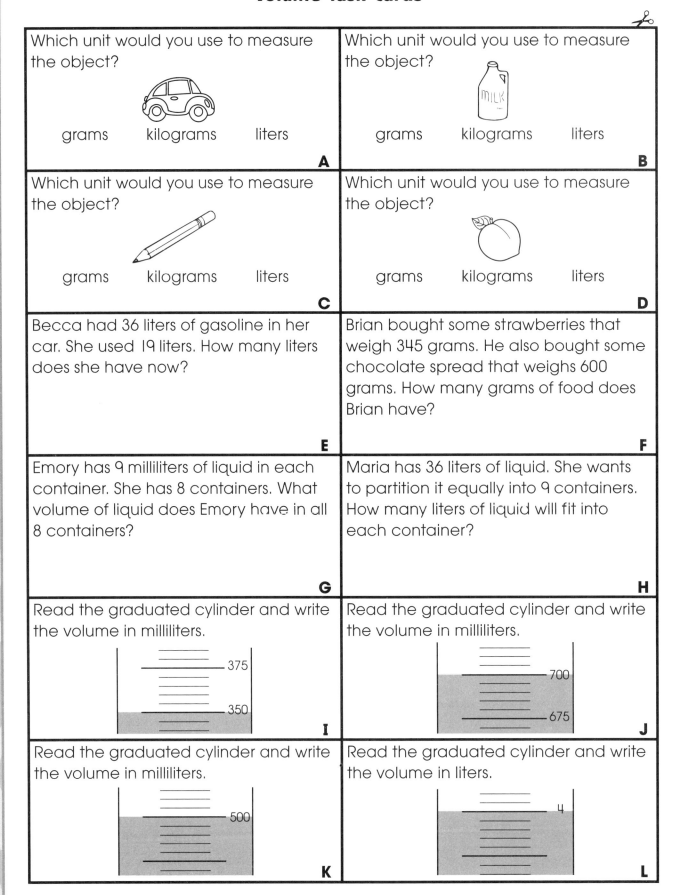

Which unit would you use to measure the object?

grams   kilograms   liters

A

Which unit would you use to measure the object?

grams   kilograms   liters

B

Which unit would you use to measure the object?

grams   kilograms   liters

C

Which unit would you use to measure the object?

grams   kilograms   liters

D

Becca had 36 liters of gasoline in her car. She used 19 liters. How many liters does she have now?

E

Brian bought some strawberries that weigh 345 grams. He also bought some chocolate spread that weighs 600 grams. How many grams of food does Brian have?

F

Emory has 9 milliliters of liquid in each container. She has 8 containers. What volume of liquid does Emory have in all 8 containers?

G

Maria has 36 liters of liquid. She wants to partition it equally into 9 containers. How many liters of liquid will fit into each container?

H

Read the graduated cylinder and write the volume in milliliters.

375

350

I

Read the graduated cylinder and write the volume in milliliters.

700

675

J

Read the graduated cylinder and write the volume in milliliters.

500

K

Read the graduated cylinder and write the volume in liters.

4

L

To prep: Copy on card stock and laminate for durability. Cut apart and place them in a center. If desired, write the answer on the back of each card to make them self-checking.

Scaled Graphs

 Essential Question

How can scaled picture and bar graphs with multiple categories be used to solve problems?

Warm-Up/Review

Ask the class, "How many of you would like pizza for lunch? How many of you would like tacos for lunch?" Record the data in a chart. Explain to students that asking questions like that is a way of gathering data or information.

 Mini-Lesson

Materials: sticky notes, chart paper

1. Give each student a sticky note. Ask each student to draw a picture of how she got to school this morning (by bus, walking, car ride, etc.) on a note. Have students randomly place the notes on the board.

2. Explain that the notes are the collected data for a graph. Now, the data needs to be organized.

3. Demonstrate how to include a title, labels for the vertical and horizontal axes, and labels for the columns. Show how to organize the data by putting the notes in categories and then placing them neatly on the graph, forming columns. Explain how using pictures and having a key to show that 1 picture equals 1 student makes this a picture graph. Explain that if they did not use pictures and a key, and just made a column it would be called a bar graph.

4. Ask, "How did the majority of students get to school? How many students rode the bus? What was the way the least amount of students came to school? If we lived in another part of the country, would our data change?"

5. Then, model creating a bar graph with a scale other than one.

Note: Take a picture of the data from this lesson to use in the Enrichment lesson.

 Math Talk

What are the benefits of using scaled graphs?
Why would you use a bar graph instead of a picture graph?
Name some other types of graphs.

 Journal Prompt

Decide on a survey topic you would like to collect data on, such as pets at home, number of siblings, favorite colors, favorite foods, etc. Collect the data and create a chart. Using the information in the chart, create a picture graph or bar graph to display your data. Write three true statements about the data on the graph.

Materials

sticky notes
chart paper
book of world records or almanac

 Workstations

Activity sheets (pages 137–139)
Graphing Cereal (page 140)

 Guided Math

◯ **Remediation: Creating a Graph**

1. Use sticky notes with the group. Have students label each note with a student's name from the class. Then, have them color the notes red (boy) or blue (girl).
2. Ask students to organize the data into categories.
3. Model how to draw a graph. Have students use the model to draw their own graphs. Add a title, label the axes, and write labels for the columns. Show how to make columns to represent the data. Explain that if the data were shown in pictures and included a key, this would be called a picture graph.
4. Ask students to make observations about the data on the graph. Say, "According to this graph, most of the kids in our class are boys. There are 4 more boys than girls. I wonder if other classes have more boys than girls."

▢ **On Level: Working with Data**

1. Bring in a book of world records or an almanac. Find an interesting topic to graph, such as fastest animals. Before they read the article, ask students to predict which animal is the fastest and how fast it can move.
2. Have students record and organize the information. Create a bar graph as a group. Study the data and decide how to best represent it. Ask, "What will the scale of the graph be? What intervals will the numbers be on the vertical axis?" Label the axes.
3. Have students look at the bar graph and make true statements about what the data shows.
4. Discuss, "Were our predictions close to the actual data? What did we learn about animals? Was there anything that surprised us about the results?"

△ **Enrichment: Representing Data**

1. Use the data from the mini-lesson. During the mini-lesson students made a picture graph. Explain that there are many ways to represent data.
2. Ask, "What other ways are there to illustrate the findings?" Discuss horizontal and vertical bar graphs, line plots, line graphs, pictographs, tally charts, and tables.
3. Create each type of graph together. Ask, "Are there some that are better than others? Can we display the information on every kind of graph? Which graphs are easier to understand? What are the pros and cons of each one? Why would someone choose one type of graph over another?"
4. On chart paper, create a poster of the various ways to represent the same data.

 Assess and Extend

Ask students to collect data and create a picture graph showing the number of boys and girls in the classroom. Use a scale of 2.

Name _____   Date _____

 Scaled Graphs   ● Creating a Graph

Use the information in each T-chart to complete a bar graph and a picture graph. Then, use the graphs to answer the questions.

Favorite School Lunch

Lunches	Number of Kids
lasagna	ℍℍ
sub sandwich	ℍℍ ||
grilled cheese	|||
pizza	ℍℍ ℍℍ

1. How many students like sub sandwiches best? _____

2. What lunch choice is the overall favorite? _____

3. What lunch choice do the fewest number of students like? _____

4. How many students were asked about their favorite school lunch?_____

Favorite Summer Activity

Activity	Number of Kids
swimming	ℍℍ ||
baseball	||||
soccer	ℍℍ
tennis	||

Key: _____

5. How many students like baseball?_____

6. What activity do most students like the best? _____

7. How many students like soccer or baseball? _____

8. What activity had the fewest number of kids who liked it?_____

Scaled Graphs

Use the information in each T-chart to complete the bar graph. Then, use the graphs to answer the questions.

Number of Kids in Each Grade

Grade Level	Number of Kids
1st grade	55
2nd grade	85
3rd grade	70
4th grade	55
5th grade	90

1. What grade has the most students? _____

2. Which grades have the same amount of students? _____

3. How many students are in either 3rd or 4th grade? _____

4. Write an observation about the data represented in the graph. _____
_____

Tickets Sold to Baseball Game

Month	Tickets Sold
May	400
June	400
July	700
August	600
September	250

Key: _____

5. Which month had the fewest tickets sold? _____

6. How many tickets were sold during June, July, and August? _____

7. Justify the scale you chose. _____

8. Write an observation about the data represented in the graph. _____
_____

Name _____   Date _____

Answer the questions. Using the data provided and your answers to the questions, draw the best type of graph to display each set of data.

Reading Choices in Library

Choices	Number of Kids
Picture Books	400
Chapter Books	750
Nonfiction	800
Magazines	150

1. What scale would be best to show this data? Why?

_____

2. Is a tally chart a good choice to display this data? Explain.

_____

3. Can this data be shown with a line plot? Why or why not?

_____

4. Would a vertical or horizontal bar graph be better? Explain.

_____

Eye Color

Color	Number of Kids
brown	卌 |||
blue	||||
green	||
hazel	||||

5. What scale would be best to show this data? Why?

_____

6. Would a table or a bar graph be more helpful to compare results? Explain.

_____

7. Could this information be plotted as a line graph? Why or why not?

_____

8. If this data were represented in a pictograph, what would be a good symbol to use?

_____

Graphing Cereal

Materials: bag of marshmallow cereal, crayons

Directions: Sort the marshmallows into categories to create a graph using the chart below. Then, color in each bar, add a title, and label the axes. On a separate sheet of paper, write and answer four questions using the data you have collected from the graph.

Rainbow	Pink Heart	Shooting Star	Red Balloon	Purple Horseshoe	Four-Leaf Clover	Pot of Gold	Blue Moon

Caution: Before beginning any food activity, ask families' permission and inquire about students' food allergies and religious or other food restrictions.

- ✂

To prep: Measure 1 to 2 cups of marshmallow cereal into individual resealable plastic bags and place in a center with copies of the chart.

Line Plots

 ## Essential Question

How can measurement data be gathered and marked on a line plot?

 ## Warm-Up/Review

Tell students to stand up when you say a number that represents how many siblings they have. For example, when you say two, the students with 2 siblings will stand up. Record the information in a tally chart. Ask, "How would you represent the data from this chart?" (bar graph or picture graph)

 ## Mini-Lesson

Materials: sticky notes

1. Give each student a sticky note and have them draw a large X on it. Explain that you are doing a survey to find how many pets students have at home. You are going to collect the data and organize it on a line plot.

2. Write the numbers 0–10 on the board low enough so that students can put their sticky notes above the numbers. Have students come to the board and place their sticky notes above the number that represents the number of pets they have at home.

3. After each student has done this, point out the numbers that show the least and the greatest number of pets. Explain that when creating a line plot, we are only using a section of a number line. Draw a number line on the board that begins with the fewest amount of pets shown and ends with the most amount of pets shown. Be sure to label all of the numbers in between. Explain to students that when creating a line plot, you have to include all of the numbers in between the least and the greatest even if there is no data for each point. Have students move their sticky notes to the space above the appropriate number on the line plot. Emphasize that the sticky notes should be placed so that they align across.

4. Discuss the graph. Ask, "What kind of information is represented on this graph? Does it tell us what kinds of pets people have? How many pets do most people have? What is the fewest number of pets people have? How many people have more than 2 pets?"

5. Have students draw the graph and write several statements about the data. Then, let students share their statements.

Note: Take a picture of the data from this lesson to use in the Enrichment lesson.

 ## Math Talk

How does using a line plot help you organize data?
What is easy to learn from this graph?
What is not easy to learn from this graph? Why?

 ## Journal Prompt

Make a list of data that you could use a line plot to organize.

Materials

dice
graph from the mini-lesson

 Workstations

Activity sheets (pages 143–145)
Line Plot Task Cards (page 146)

 Guided Math

⬤ **Remediation: Representing Line Plot Data**
1. Draw a tally chart labeled *Favorite Number* (0, 1, 2, 3, 4, 5, 6, 7, 8, 9) and *Number of Teachers* (in tallies: 4, 3, 1, 6, 3, 2, 0, 6, 3, 2). Explain that you surveyed the teachers, and these are their favorite numbers.
2. Draw a number line labeled from 0–9. Title it *Teachers' Favorite Numbers*. Assign each student a number along the number line and have him draw the correct number of *X*s above his number based on the information in the tally chart.
3. Discuss the completed line plot. Ask questions such as, "Which number or numbers did most teachers like best? Did more teachers like 2 or 9? Were there any numbers that no teachers chose?"
4. Ask students to draw the line plot. Emphasize having a title, evenly spacing the numbers on a horizontal line, and drawing the Xs directly above one another and aligning them horizontally.

⬜ **On Level: Collecting Line Plot Data**
1. Draw a number line labeled with numbers from 1–6. Let students take turns rolling a die and drawing an X on the line plot to record the results of their rolls. Roll the die at least 10 times.
2. Ask questions such as, "How many times did we roll 5? Were there any numbers we didn't roll at all? How many times did we roll in all? How many times did you roll 4 or more? How many times did you roll a number greater than 4?"
3. Have students repeat the experiment on their own and record 10 rolls on a line plot. Ask students to write their own questions about the data they just plotted. Have them trade their questions with a partner and answer their partner's questions using her line plot.

△ **Enrichment: Analyzing Line Plot Data**
1. Use the graph from the mini-lesson to gather and analyze data. First, have the group draw the line plot.
2. Introduce *range* (difference between the greatest number and the least number), *mode* (the number that occurs most often), *median* (the middle number when the data is arranged from least to greatest), *gaps* (spaces or blanks in the data), and *outliers* (any data that is outside the range of most of the data).
3. Use the data from the graph to find each of these statistics. Then, have students use the information to analyze the data. Ask, "What is an outlier? What can a gap tell us about the data?"
4. Discuss how using a line plot makes analyzing data easier.

 Assess and Extend

Draw a tally chart on the board labeled *Amount of Snow* (0, 1/4 inch, 1/2 inch, 3/4 inch, 1 inch) and *Frequency* (in tallies: 11, 3, 7, 4, 6). Have students make a line plot to show the data.

Line Plots   ● Representing Line Plot Data

Show the data on each line plot. Then, use the line plots to answer the questions.

Ages of Kids in Class

Age	Kids
7	I
8	ℍ II
9	ℍ I
10	II

1. How many students are 8 years old? _____

2. What age are the least number of students? _____

3. What age are the greatest number of students? _____

4. How many 8- and 9-year-olds are there in this class? _____

Class Quiz Scores

Points	Kids
0	
1	I
2	I
3	IIII
4	ℍ I
5	ℍ III

5. What number of points did no students score? _____

6. How many students scored 3 or fewer points? _____

7. How many more students scored 4 points than 1 point? _____

8. How many students are in this class altogether? _____

143

Line Plots   ☐ Collecting Line Plot Data

Shuffle a set of 0–9 number cards. Place them facedown and draw a card at random. Record your result on the line plot. Replace the card and repeat 20 times. Answer the questions about your line plot.

1. Write a title for your line plot in the space provided.

2. What number was drawn the least?

_____

3. What number was drawn the most?

_____

4. How many times did you draw an even number?

_____

5. Were any numbers never drawn?

_____

6. How many times did you draw a number greater than 6?

_____

7. How many times did you draw 4 or less?

_____

8. How can showing data in a line plot make answering these questions easier?

_____

_____

_____

Name _____   **Date** _____

Think of a survey question to ask the class, such as, "How many people live in your house?" If a survey is not possible, research a question such as, "How many pages do the fiction books in the classroom contain?" Collect data in the tally chart. Then, organize the data on a line plot graph. Use the line plot to answer the questions about the data. Write three observations about the data.

1. Survey question: _____

_____

2. What was the most popular answer? _____

What was the least popular answer? _____

How many data points did you collect in all? *Hint:* How many Xs are on your

line plot? _____

What were the greatest and least numbers you collected? _____

3. Observations about the data:

_____

_____

_____

Line Plot Task Cards

Crayons Used in the Classroom

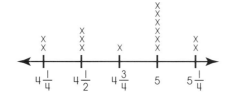

How many crayons measured less than 5 inches?

A

Fish in the Pond

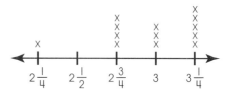

How many fish measured longer than $2\frac{1}{2}$ inches?

B

Paintbrushes in the Art Room

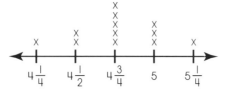

How many total paintbrushes were in the art room?

C

Sticks in the Yard

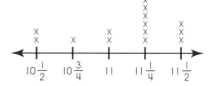

How many more sticks measured $11\frac{1}{4}$ inches than $10\frac{1}{2}$ inches?

D

Ladybugs in the Jar

$1\frac{1}{4}$ in.	2
$1\frac{1}{2}$ in.	1
$2\frac{1}{4}$ in.	5

Use the information in the chart to create a line plot.

E

Watches in the Store

$9\frac{1}{4}$ in.	5
$9\frac{1}{2}$ in.	0
$10\frac{1}{4}$ in.	3

Use the information in the chart to create a line plot.

F

Students' Block Towers

$8\frac{1}{2}$ in.	5
$9\frac{1}{4}$ in.	3
$9\frac{1}{2}$ in.	6

Use the information in the chart to create a line plot.

G

Lengths of Ribbons

$6\frac{1}{4}$ in.	7
$7\frac{1}{2}$ in.	1
$7\frac{3}{4}$ in.	4

Use the information in the chart to create a line plot.

H

Lengths of Pieces of String

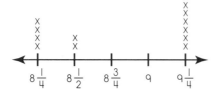

Write a question that can be answered using the data in the line plot above.

I

Paper Clips in the Drawer

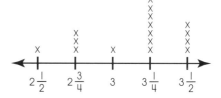

Write a question that can be answered using the data in the line plot above.

J

To prep: If desired, copy the task cards on card stock and laminate for durability. Place them in a math station. Answers should be recorded on a separate sheet of paper.

 # Area

 Essential Question

What is area?
How can area be measured?

 Warm-Up/Review

Say, "When we say something is 'large,' what does that mean?" Draw some rectangles on the board, some larger than others. Ask, "How do you find the largest rectangle? What does 'largest' mean?"

 Mini-Lesson

Materials: square tiles, centimeter graph paper

1. Give each student square tiles. Ask them to get creative and build any size rectangle using the square tiles provided. *Note:* Students should make a filled rectangle, not an outline. Once they have finished, ask them to count the number of square tiles they used. Explain that the amount they counted is the *area*, or the space the rectangle covers. Repeat a few more times with different sized rectangles.

2. Next, give each student a sheet of graph paper. Explain that each square on the paper is 1 centimeter tall by 1 centimeter wide. Have students draw the following rectangles on their graph paper: *5 x 1, 4 x 2, 3 x 3*.

3. Ask students to count the squares in each rectangle. The area unit is square centimeters because you are counting the entire square, and the square's length and width are 1 centimeter. Record the area for each rectangle (for example, *A (area) = 5 square centimeters*).

4. Have students practice with a partner. One student should draw a rectangle on the graph paper and challenge his partner to find the area. Switch and repeat several times.

 Math Talk

Which rectangle has the greatest area? How do you know?
When would you need to find area in the real world?
What are other ways to find area?

 Journal Prompt

Write the definition of *area* in your own words. You can use pictures to help you explain.

Materials

square tiles
geoboards
rubber bands
dice
graph paper

 Workstations

Activity sheets (pages 149–151)
Dicey Area (page 152)

 Guided Math

○ **Remediation: Working with Tiles**

1. Ask each student to use square tiles to create a rectangular array that is 3 x 4. Ask, "How many blocks are in this rectangle? This space it covers is the area. What is the area?" (12 square inches)

2. Draw a picture of the rectangle, including the divisions inside. Show students how to count the inside squares to find the area.

3. Continue working with the square tiles. Ask students to find an area: "Show me a rectangle with an area of 20 square inches." Have students show their squares and explain how they know their rectangles are 20 square inches and share the strategies they used to create the rectangles. Discuss how different rectangles can have the same area.

□ **On Level: Area with Geoboards**

1. Explain to students that they will be finding different ways to show square units for area on a geoboard. Demonstrate how to show a 5 x 2 area on a geoboard.

2. Pair students together. Give each student a geoboard, some rubber bands, and two dice. The first student rolls both dice and adds together the numbers. The student should build a shape on her geoboard with an area that equals the sum of the dice. Have her give her geoboard to a partner to check her work. Repeat with the second student for the next round.

3. Discuss the different shapes students are making. Have them discuss why some areas might be the same, even though the shapes look different. Have students share their shapes and strategies for creating rectangles with specific areas.

△ **Enrichment: Word Problems Involving Area**

1. Provide students access to graph paper, square tiles, and geoboards with rubber bands. Show the following problem: *The art teacher Mrs. Ross wants students to paint a mural on a blank school wall in the building. She marks off a rectangular area 4 meters long by 3 meters wide. What is the area of this mural?* (12 sq. m)

2. Explain to students that they can use whatever materials provided to solve the problem. When students find the solution, have them share their answer and explain how they solved the problem.

3. Continue practicing with other problems, such as: *Mrs. Ross marks an area of 32 square meters for the mural in the gym. If the length of this mural is 8 meters, what is the width of the mural?* (4 m)

 Assess and Extend

Write the names of different rectangular objects found in the classroom on separate sticky notes. For example, *books, tissue boxes, crayon boxes, dry-erase boards*, etc. Place students in pairs and give each pair a sticky note and inch blocks. Have them find the area of their object using the inch blocks and explain how they did it.

Name _____ Date ____

● Workin

Name

Find the area of each figure.

1.

A = _____

2.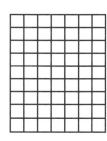

A = _____

3.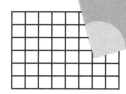

A = _____

4.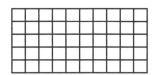

A = _____

5.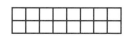

A = _____

6.

A = _____

7.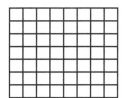

A = _____

8.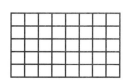

A = _____

9.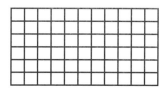

A = _____

10.

A = _____

11.

A = _____

12.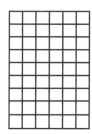

A = _____

13.

A = _____

14.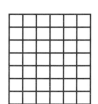

A = _____

15.

A = _____

You can use a geoboard to find the area of a figure. Use a rubber band to mark the outline of the figure. Then, count the squares inside the figure to determine the area.

1.

A = _____

2.
A = _____

3.
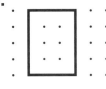
A = _____

4.

A = _____

5.
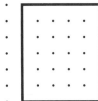
A = _____

6.
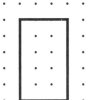
A = _____

7.
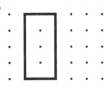
A = _____

8.
A = _____

9.
A = _____

10.
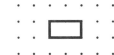
A = _____

Name _____   Date _____

 **Area**   ▲ Word Problems Involving Area

Solve. Use graph paper, inch blocks, and/or geoboards to help you. Show your work.

1. The Quimby brothers are painting a wall in their living room. The wall measures 7 feet by 9 feet. What is the area of the wall?

2. Wendy is putting carpet down in a room that measures 8 feet long by 11 feet wide. What is the area of the room?

3. The zoo is building a new rhino pool that will measure 60 meters by 8 meters. What is the area of the pool?

4. The Hoffmans' deck is almost finished. Each side of the square deck is 10 feet long. What was the area of the deck?

5. The college donated land for a park. The land was 80 meters by 7 meters wide. What is the area of the land?

6. Elliot digs a flower bed that is 6 meters long by 5 meters wide. What is the area of the flower bed?

7. Carmon wants to tile her kitchen floor. How many 1-foot tiles will she need if her floor is 12 feet long by 10 feet wide?

Dicey Area

Materials: 2 different colored pencils or dry-erase markers, deck of cards (face cards removed)

To play: Shuffle the cards and place facedown. Players take turns drawing two cards. Create an area model with the two numbers as the length and width. (*Note*: Aces are equal to 1.) Find the area of the rectangle or square and shade it in with your color, writing the area in the center. Play continues until there is no more room left to draw or until time is up. The winner is the player who has covered the most area with their color.

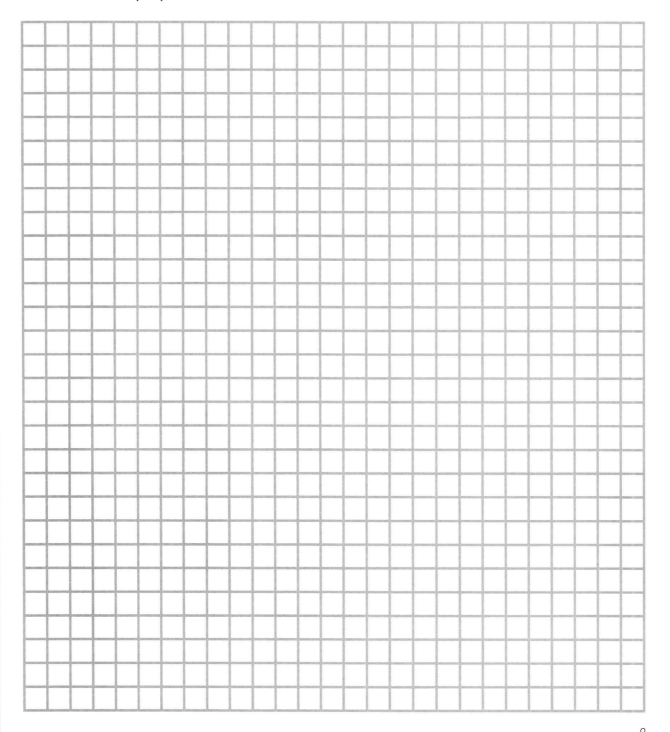

To prep: If desired, copy the gameboard on card stock and laminate for durability and so it can be used with dry-erase markers. Cut off these directions before copying.

Relating Area to Multiplication

 Essential Question

How can multiplying side lengths help to find the area of a plane figure?

 Warm-Up/Review

Review finding area using square tiles. Have students create a 4 x 3 array using square tiles. Then, have them find the area by counting all of the blocks used to make the rectangle.

 Mini-Lesson

Materials: graph paper

1. Give students graph paper. Ask them to draw all of the possible rectangles with an area of 12. (2 x 6, 6 x 2, 3 x 4, 4 x 3, 1 x 12, 12 x 1)

2. Observe students' strategies as they work. Are they counting each square unit or are they multiplying the outside lengths?

3. Model by drawing a 3 x 4 rectangle on the board (tile it appropriately inside). Explain and show that the length is 3 square units and the width is 4 square units. Point out that 3 and 4 are both factors of 12. Therefore, length times width equals area (3 x 4 = 12). Model another option by drawing a 2 x 6 rectangle on the board and demonstrating the multiplication sentence and factors for this rectangle.

4. Draw some more rectangles on the board and label them. Have students multiply to find the area of each one and give the related multiplication sentence for each.

5. Then, move to rectangles labeled with only one width or one length and squares with no sides labeled. Lead students to think critically about finding unknown numbers and what they know about the sides of a square to find the missing lengths and widths.

 Math Talk

Is it easier to multiply to find the area or to count the square units?
How can you find area if you do not know your multiplication facts?
What is the missing length/width of this side?

 Journal Prompt

Draw two different sized rectangles and find the area of both. Compare the rectangles' areas and explain which one is larger.

Materials

(none)

 Workstations

Activity sheets (pages 155–157)
Deck the Area (page 158)
Dicey Area (page 152)

 Guided Math

○ **Remediation: Finding Area by Tiling**

1. Draw a rectangle and label one side *9 ft.* and another side *4 ft.*
2. Explain that with the labeled sides, you can divide the shape into the given amount of rows and columns to "tile" the shape and find the area. Tiling also shows the array of the figure.
3. Say, "Since I know that this side is 9 feet, I can divide this shape into 9 columns." Draw 9 columns on the rectangle. "I know this side is 4 feet, so I can divide this shape into 4 rows." Draw 4 rows. "Now, I can count the tiles to determine the area." Count the tiles to find 36 tiles. "This rectangle has an area of 36 square feet."
4. Point out how the figure they drew in step 3 is like an array and explain to students they can multiply the length and width of the rectangle to find the area instead of counting all of the tiles. Write the multiplication sentence *9 × 4 = 36* next to the rectangle.
5. Continue having students practice with other rectangles and squares.

□ **On Level: Finding Real World Area**

1. Read students the following problem: *Brian is painting an accent wall in his bedroom. The wall measures 12 feet by 9 feet. Brian needs to find the area of the wall to determine how much paint to buy. What is the area of Brian's accent wall?*
2. Explain that sometimes drawing a picture is helpful in understanding word problems. Draw a rectangle. Label the rectangle with *12 feet* and *9 feet*. Ask, "What do I need to do to find the area?" (multiply the length times the width, or 12 × 9)
3. Say, "Twelve times 9 equals 108, and since we know it is measured in feet, the area of Brian's accent wall is 108 square feet."
4. Continue practicing with other real-world examples of finding area.

△ **Enrichment: Finding Missing Side Lengths**

1. Draw a rectangle and label the length *8 cm* and the width with a question mark. Above the rectangle, write *A = 56 square cm*.
2. Ask students, "How do I find the missing length width of this rectangle?" Have students share their thoughts about what to do to find the width.
3. Explain that you can use the formula for area to help you find the missing width. The formula for area is *A = length × width*. So, you can plug in the numbers that you know into the formula. Record *56 = 8 × ?*.
4. Tell students you can divide the area by the given length to determine the missing width. Model setting up and solving 56 ÷ 8 = 7 to find that the width of the rectangle is 7 cm.
5. Draw another rectangle with a width labeled *5 cm* and a missing length. Write *A = 45 square cm* above the rectangle. Ask students to solve for the missing length. Have students share their answers and how they solved for the missing length. (9 cm)
6. Continue to have students practice with different rectangles by giving them the area for the figure and only one side length.

 Assess and Extend

Draw and label the following figures on the board: 5 x 9 rectangle; 7 x 7 square; 9 x 3 rectangle. Have students find each area and explain in words or pictures how they found the answer.

Name _____   Date _____

Relating Area to Multiplication ● Finding Area by Tiling

Find the area using tiling and multiplication.

1.

5 in.
3 in.

A = _____

2.

4 ft.
4 ft.

A = _____

3.

8 ft.
2 ft.

A = _____

4.
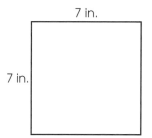
7 in.
7 in.

A = _____

5.

9 in.
5 in.

A = _____

6.
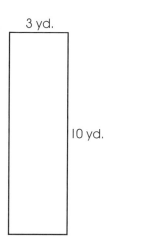
3 yd.
10 yd.

A = _____

7.

4 m
4 m

A = _____

8.
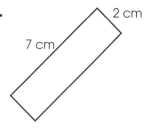
2 cm
7 cm

A = _____

9.
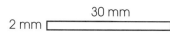
30 mm
2 mm

A = _____

10.
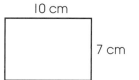
10 cm
7 cm

A = _____

11.
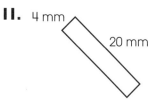
4 mm
20 mm

A = _____

12.
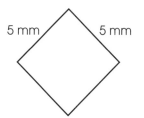
5 mm   5 mm

A = _____

Relating Area to Multiplication ■ Finding Real World Area

Find the area for each problem.

1. Ella wants to make tiled coasters for her living room. The base of the coaster is 4 inches by 4 inches. She wants to glue on 1 inch tiles. How many 1 inch tiles is Ella going to need for each coaster?

4 in.
4 in.

2. The city is painting a billboard downtown. The billboard measures 20 meters long by 9 meters tall. The city needs to find the area of the billboard to determine how much paint they will need. What is the area of the billboard?

9 m
20 m

3. Jordan wants to put carpet in his guest bedroom. The floor measures 10 feet by 9 feet. How much carpet will Jordan need to buy?

9 ft.
10 ft.

4. The school wants to re-tile the classrooms in the third-grade hallway. Each classroom measures 10 yards by 9 yards. What is the area of each third-grade classroom?

9 yd.
10 yd.

5. Luke is planting a garden for his mom. It is 6 meters by 8 meters. Luke must find the area to determine how many flowers he can fit in the garden. What is the area of Luke's garden?

6 m
5 m

6. Shannon needs to find how much wallpaper to use to cover one wall. The wall is 7 feet long by 8 feet tall. How many square feet of wallpaper will Shannon need?

8 ft.
7 ft.

7. Perry is helping his uncle build a tree house. The floor of the tree house is going to measure 5 feet by 6 feet. What will the area of Perry's tree house be?

6 ft.
5 ft.

Challenge: Ivy is looking for a rug for her living room. Her living room has an area of 90 square feet. She finds a rug that is 10 ft. long. How many feet wide does it need to be to be able to cover Ivy's entire living room?

156

Relating Area to Multiplication ▲ Finding Missing Side Lengths

Find the missing height or length for each rectangle. Write the division problem you used to show your work.

I. A = 30 sq. cm

6 cm

?

? = _____

_____

2. A = 4 sq. cm

2 cm

?

? = _____

_____

3. A = 30 sq. ft.

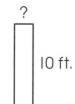

?

10 ft.

? = _____

_____

4. A = 16 sq. in.

?

4 in.

? = _____

_____

5. A = 60 sq. ft.

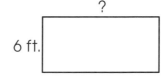

?

6 ft.

? = _____

_____

6. A = 21 sq. cm

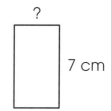

?

7 cm

? = _____

_____

7. A = 40 sq. in

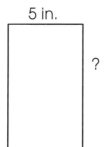

5 in.

?

? = _____

_____

8. A = 560 sq. cm

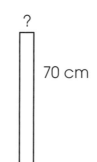

?

70 cm

? = _____

_____

9. A = 99 sq. m

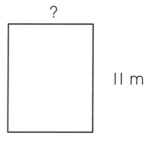

?

11 m

? = _____

_____

Deck the Area

Materials: deck of cards (face cards removed)

To play: Draw two cards from the deck. Draw an area model using the numbers from the cards as your length and width. (*Note*: Aces are equal to 1.) Write the equation for each area model and solve.

My Area Models and Equations	

Additive Area

 Essential Question

What strategies can be used to find the areas of rectilinear figures?

 Warm-Up/Review

Review how to find the area of a rectangle. Draw a rectangle on the board and label it 3 inches by 5 inches. Have students find the area and explain the strategy they used to find the area.

 Mini-Lesson

Materials: centimeter graph paper

1. Draw an irregular, rectilinear figure with multiple sides and angles on graph paper. A good example is the block letter *E*. Ask, "How do I find the area of this shape?" Model counting the blocks.

2. Draw a similar irregular figure on plain paper. Label the sides. Ask, "How can we find the area?" Show students how to divide irregular figures into rectangular sections. Explain that this is helpful because they already know how to find the areas of rectangles. Find the areas of the smaller sections and add them together to find the total area of the irregular figure.

3. Show different ways to divide the figure and emphasize that there is not a wrong way, as long as the pieces are all rectangles.

4. Continue to practice finding the areas of other irregular shapes. Have students share their different strategies.

 Math Talk

Why do you divide the irregular figures into rectangles to find the area?

When might you need to find the area of something in the real world that is irregularly shaped?

How else could you find the area of an irregular shape?

 Journal Prompt

Draw your own irregular figures, label the sides, and trade with a partner to find the area.

Materials

copies of irregular figures
dry-erase pockets
colored dry-erase markers
sticky notes (optional)
centimeter graph paper

 Workstations

Activity sheets (pages 161–163)
Irregular Area Three-in-a-Row
(page 164)
Dicey Area (page 152)
Deck the Area (page 158)

 Guided Math

⚪ **Remediation: Dividing Irregular Figures**

1. Place the copies of irregular figures in dry-erase pockets. Explain, "It is easier to find the areas of irregular figures if we break them into rectangles." Sketch one of the irregular figures and model one way to draw lines and divide it into rectangles. Have students use dry-erase markers to divide the same figure a different way on their dry-erase pocket. It may be helpful for some students to use sticky notes to cover certain parts of a figure to better see the smaller rectangles.

2. Demonstrate how to find the area of each rectangle, and add the areas to find the total area of the figure. Repeat with the same figure divided in a different way. Emphasize that there is more than one way to divide most irregular figures, but that the final area should always be the same.

3. Practice with several more irregular figures on the page. Allow students to share the different ways they divided the figure and the area they found.

4. Have students draw their own figures on centimeter graph paper and trade with a partner to divide and find the area.

🟦 **On Level: Tiling Irregular Figures**

1. Draw an irregular figure and label the sides. Demonstrate how to divide the irregular shape into rectangular sections.

2. Explain to students that you can tile the inside of each of the rectangular sections to help you find the area. Demonstrate how to divide the rectangular sections into rows and columns based on their labels and then count the tiles.

3. Draw another irregular figure. Have students divide it into rectangular sections. Have them explain how to divide the sections into rows and columns to find the area.

4. Continue to practice by having students draw their own irregular figures and find the area by tiling. Have students move to using multiplication when ready.

🔺 **Enrichment: Using Subtraction to Find Area**

1. Draw an irregular figure and label the sides. Demonstrate using another color or a dotted line to extend the outermost edges to make the irregular figure a whole rectangular figure.

2. Find the area of the whole rectangle. Then, model how to find the area of the smaller rectangular figure (or figures) that you added to the original figure with your other color. *Note:* It may be helpful to shade these figures a different color to set them apart from the original shape.

3. Explain that when you subtract the area of the smaller figure(s) from the area of the total figure, you can find the area of the original irregular figure.

4. Continue to practice finding the areas of other irregular figures.

 Assess and Extend

Sketch an L-shaped figure and label it with measurements of your choosing. Have students solve the following problem: *Jarvis has a closet shaped like the figure shown. He wants to put two different kinds of flooring in his closet. Each section of flooring should be a rectangle to make installation easy. He has chosen a tile that is $2 per square foot and a carpet that is $1 per square foot. Describe how Jarvis can cover his closet floor in the cheapest way.*

Additive Area

● Dividing Irregular Figures

Draw lines to divide each figure into rectangles. Then, find the area of each figure.

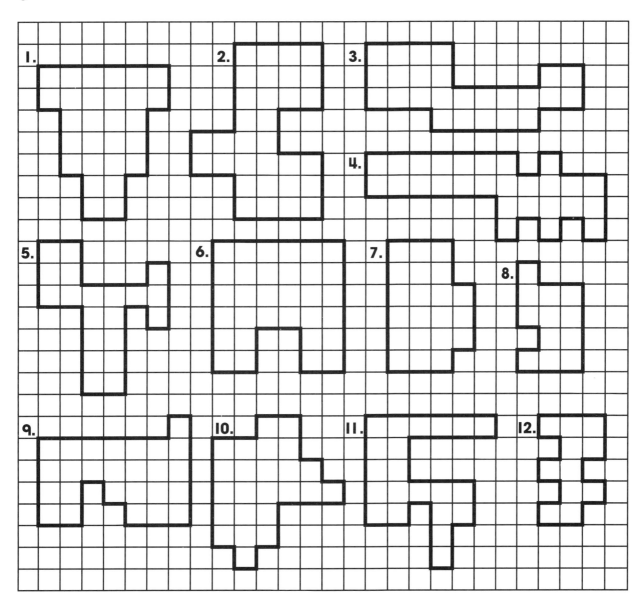

1. A = _____ sq. units

2. A = _____ sq. units

3. A = _____ sq. units

4. A = _____ sq. units

5. A = _____ sq. units

6. A = _____ sq. units

7. A = _____ sq. units

8. A = _____ sq. units

9. A = _____ sq. units

10. A = _____ sq. units

11. A = _____ sq. units

12. A = _____ sq. units

Additive Area   ■ **Tiling Irregular Figures**

Find the area of each figure.

I.

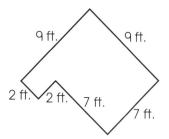

A = _____

2.

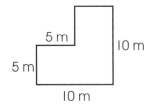

A = _____

3.

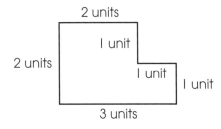

A = _____

4.

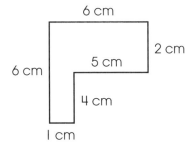

A = _____

5.

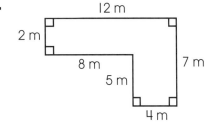

A = _____

6.

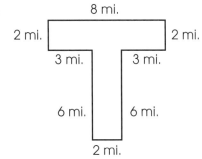

A = _____

Name _____   Date _____

Find the area of each figure. Write the equations using the subtraction method below each problem.

1.

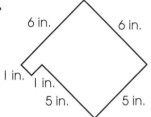

A = _____

2.

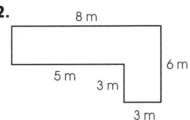

A = _____

3.

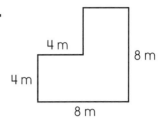

A = _____

4.

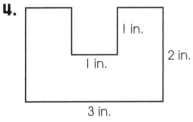

A = _____

5.

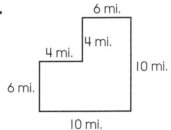

A = _____

6.

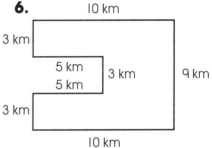

A = _____

7.

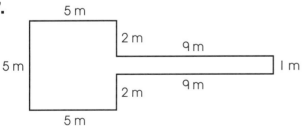

A = _____

8.

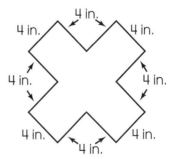

A = _____

Irregular Area Three-in-a-Row

Materials: two-color counters or dry-erase markers

To play: Players take turns. Find the area of the irregular figure in the space. If you solve it correctly, use a counter to cover the space or draw an X or O with a dry-erase marker. The first player to cover three spaces in a row wins.

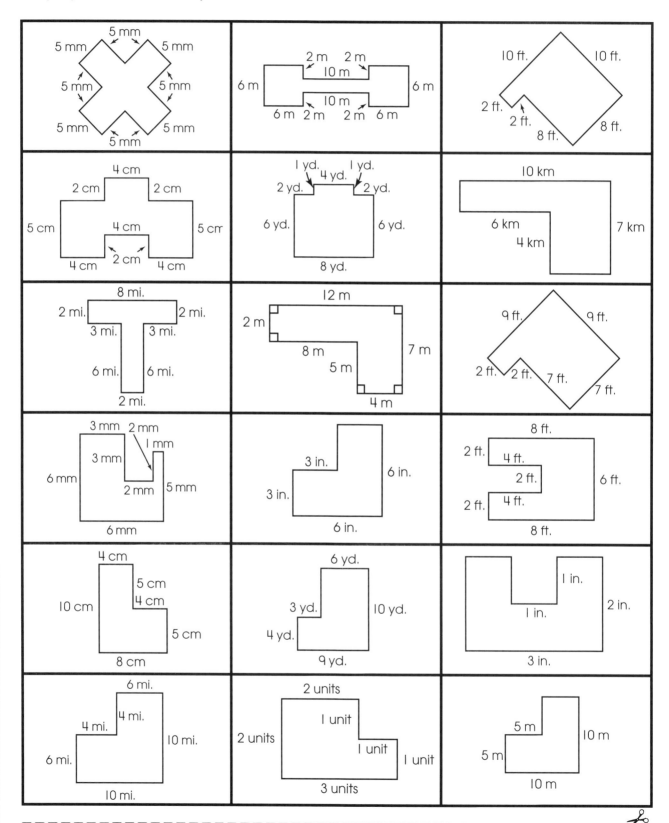

Perimeter

 Essential Question

How do you find the perimeters of shapes?

 Warm-Up/Review

Review with students what area is and brainstorm what kinds of things in life we measure using area (paint for walls, carpets for flooring, etc.). Make a list of all the things students come up with.

 Mini-Lesson

Materials: centimeter graph paper

1. Give each student a sheet of graph paper. Explain that each square on the paper is 1 centimeter by 1 centimeter. Show students a drawing on the graph paper of a 5 x 1 rectangle.

2. Ask, "If you start at one corner of the rectangle and walk all the way around it along the border, how far would you walk?" Ask students to draw and label the rectangle. Count the outside units of the rectangle and show how it adds up to 12 centimeters. Explain that this is the *perimeter* of the rectangle, or the distance around it. Write next to the rectangle *P (perimeter) = 12*.

3. Have students draw a 4 x 2 rectangle on the graph paper. Ask them to find the perimeter of this rectangle. Discuss how and why this shape and the one in steps 1 and 2 have the same perimeter, but different shapes.

4. Have students practice finding perimeter with a partner. One student should draw a rectangle and have their partner find the perimeter. Switch and repeat.

 Math Talk

When would you need to find perimeter in
  the real world?
What are other ways to find perimeter?
How are perimeter and area related?

 Journal Prompt

Write the definition of *perimeter* in your own words. You can use pictures to help you explain.

Materials

square tiles
yarn
centimeter graph paper
blank paper

 Workstations

Activity sheets (pages 167–169)
Perimeter Task Cards (page 170)

 Guided Math

⬤ **Remediation: Working with Tiles**
   1. Ask each student to use square tiles to create a rectangular array that is 5 x 3. Have students take a piece of yarn and wrap it around the outside of the figure. Then, straighten the yarn out and place tiles along the piece of yarn to determine how many tiles are equal to the length of the yarn. Say, "The distance around is 16 tiles long. This rectangle has a perimeter of 16 inches."
   2. Draw a picture of the rectangle and label it with the side lengths. Show students how to add the side lengths to find the perimeter.
   3. Continue working with the square tiles. Ask students to find the perimeter of each rectangle they create using either method.

⬜ **On Level: Calculating Perimeter**
   1. Give students graph paper. Ask them to draw all of the possible rectangles with a perimeter of 18 centimeters. (1 x 8, 2 x 7, 3 x 6, 4 x 5)
   2. Observe students' strategies as they work. Are they counting each tile or writing number sentences? After drawing, ask students to explain their strategies and write equations to calculate the perimeter, such as *1 + 8 + 1 + 8.*
   3. Draw some rectangles on plain paper and label them to find perimeter. Include rectangles with only one width and one length and squares with only one side labeled.
   4. Discuss students' strategies for finding the perimeters and missing side lengths.

△ **Enrichment: Finding Perimeter of Irregular Figures**
   1. Draw an irregular figure with multiple sides and angles on graph paper. A good example is a block letter *F.* Ask students to determine the perimeter of the shape.
   2. Draw a similar irregular figure on plain paper. Label a few of the sides, but not all of them. Ask, "What do you need to know to find the perimeter of this shape? How can the given measurements help you determine the missing ones?" Help students add, subtract, and compare the known measurements to find all of the side lengths and calculate the perimeter of the shape.
   3. Challenge students to draw their own irregular figures, label only a few sides, and trade with partners to solve for perimeter and area.

 Assess and Extend

Ask students to explain in their own words and with pictures the difference between perimeter and area.

Perimeter   ● Working with Tiles

Find the perimeter of each rectangle.

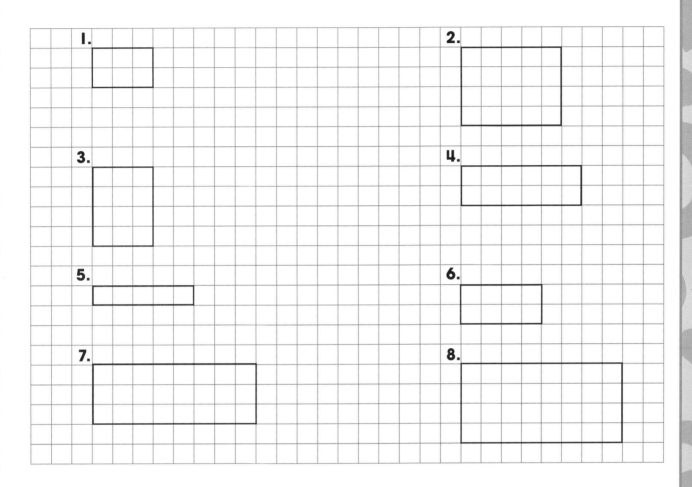

1. P = _____ units   **2.** P = _____ units

3. P = _____ units   **4.** P = _____ units

5. P = _____ units   **6.** P = _____ units

7. P = _____ units   **8.** P = _____ units

Name _____   **Date** _____

 Perimeter   ☐ Calculating Perimeter

I. Draw all of the possible rectangles that have a perimeter of 24.

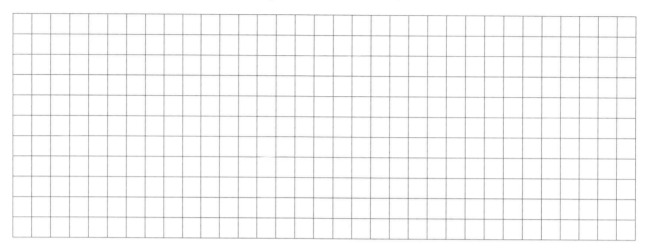

2. Draw all of the possible rectangles that have a perimeter of 30.

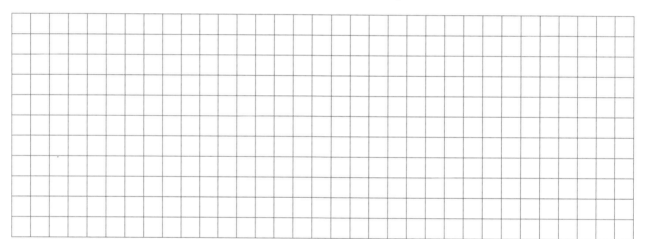

Calculate the perimeter of each rectangle.

3. P = _____

3 cm

5 cm   5 cm

3 cm

4. P = _____

9 mm

4 mm

5. P = _____

4 in.

2 in.   2 in.

4 in.

6. P = _____

7 ft.

7 ft.

Name _____   Date _____

 Perimeter   ▲ Finding Perimeter of Irregular Figures

Find the perimeter of each figure.

1.

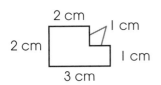

P = _____

2.

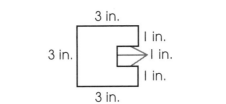

P = _____

3.

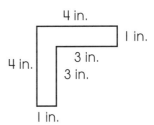

P = _____

4.

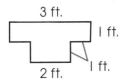

P = _____

5.

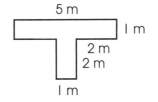

P = _____

6.

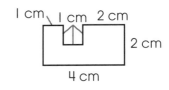

P = _____

7.

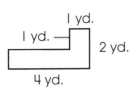

P = _____

8.

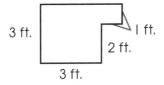

P = _____

9.

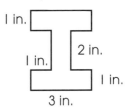

P = _____

Perimeter Task Cards

Find the perimeter.

12 mm

9 mm

A

Find the perimeter.

6 in.

7 in.

B

Find the perimeter.

6 ft.

3 ft.

C

Find the perimeter.

9 mm

3 mm

D

Find the missing side if P = 40 inches.

9 in.

E

Find the missing side if P = 50 mm.

9 mm   9 mm

14 mm

F

Find the missing side.
P = 36 ft.

12 ft.

12 ft.

G

Find the perimeter.

3 cm

H

A pentagon has sides that are all 7 millimeters long. What is the perimeter?

I

A square picture frame has sides that are 13 inches each. What is the perimeter?

J

Find the perimeter.

2 cm

1 cm

2 cm

2 cm

2 cm

K

A flower bed is rectangular. The perimeter is 36 feet. It is 8 feet wide. How long is the flower bed?

L

To prep: If desired, copy the task cards on card stock and laminate for durability. Place them in a station with centimeter graph paper.

Quadrilaterals

 ## Essential Question

How can attributes help to identify, define, and categorize quadrilaterals?

 ## Warm-Up/Review

Have students draw as many polygons as they can think of in 30 seconds. Then, have them share their polygons with the class.

 ## Mini-Lesson

Materials: chart paper, pattern blocks

1. On chart paper, create a poster with the vocabulary words for this lesson: *trapezoid*, *rhombus*, *square*, *parallelogram*, *rectangle*, *sides*, *vertices*, and *parallel*. Use the vocabulary words throughout the lesson and encourage students to use the correct terminology.

2. Ask each student to choose a pattern block of one of the shapes listed on the chart paper. Discuss each shape's attributes.

3. Create a quadrilateral poster with students. Draw a sketch of each quadrilateral on the poster. Label the sides and vertices. Write words to describe them, such as *parallel sides*, *equal length*, and *right angles*. Reference places that these shapes are seen in everyday life. Have students draw sketches and take notes.

4. Ask, "What do all of the shapes on this poster have in common?" Students should be able to see that they all have four sides. Discuss how a polygon with four sides is called a *quadrilateral*.

 ## Math Talk

What kind of quadrilateral do you see most often? Least often?
What attributes do all quadrilaterals share?
Name a quadrilateral. What makes it a quadrilateral?

 ## Journal Prompt

Draw each of the different quadrilaterals you learned about. Below each one, write the attributes that make it unique.

Materials

pattern blocks
paper bag
index cards
dry-erase boards
dry-erase markers

 Workstations

Activity sheets (pages 173–175)
Quadrilateral Bump (page 176)

 Guided Math

⚪ **Remediation: Noticing Details**

1. Give each student a trapezoid pattern block. Ask students to spend three minutes writing about their blocks. Ask, "What do you notice about the trapezoid? How many sides and vertices does it have? What makes it unique from other quadrilaterals?"

2. As students write, observe the vocabulary they use and their level of detail. Use words such as *parallel sides*, *vertices*, and *congruent* during a discussion. After the discussion, ask students to write for three more minutes using correct terminology. Repeat the same activity with other quadrilaterals.

3. Place all of the blocks in a paper bag. Pull out one shape without letting the group see. Use geometric vocabulary to describe it and have students guess the shape.

◻ **On Level: Geometric Vocabulary**

1. For many students, the most difficult part of geometry is learning the vocabulary. Many of these words are not used in everyday conversation (*parallel*, *quadrilateral*, *vertex*, etc.). So, it is important to reinforce the vocabulary by saying it, hearing it, and seeing it.

2. Have students create a set of vocabulary flash cards. Write each vocabulary word on one side of an index card and draw a sketch and write a short description of the word on the other side. For example, *4 equal sides* and *no right angles* for a rhombus.

3. Have students study their cards and quiz each other. Then, use vocabulary words to give them step-by-step directions to draw shapes. For example, say, "Draw a shape that has four sides." Students may not all draw the same shape. Then, give another direction: "This shape has four right angles." Students should change their shapes to reflect the new information. Continue until all of the details are given. Check students' drawings to see if they drew the correct shape.

△ **Enrichment: Diagramming Attributes**

1. Ask students to draw three large overlapping circles to form a triple Venn diagram. Have them refer to the vocabulary words used during the mini-lesson and on the poster. Have students choose three attributes, such as *parallel lines*, *congruent sides*, and *right angles*, and label each circle with one of the attributes.

2. Have students write the names of the quadrilaterals that fit into each category inside the circles. Quadrilaterals that fit into more than one category should be written inside the overlapping sections.

3. Have students continue making diagrams with other attributes.

4. Have students share their diagrams when they are complete. Discuss any misconceptions that arise.

 Assess and Extend

Have students draw a three column, six row table. Label each row with the following: *quadrilateral*, *parallelogram*, *square*, *rectangle*, *trapezoid*, and *rhombus*. Label each column with the following: *relationship of opposite sides*, *relationship of adjacent sides*, and *relationship of angles*. Have students complete the table with a partner. (*Note*: You may need to define *adjacent* for students.)

Quadrilaterals   ● Noticing Details

Draw a line to match each quadrilateral to its name.

1.   trapezoid

2.

3.    square

4.

5.   rhombus

6.

7.   parallelogram

8.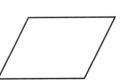

                                      rectangle

9.

Name _____   Date _____

Quadrilaterals   ■ Geometric Vocabulary

Solve each riddle by writing the name of the matching polygon. Not all words will be used.

Word Bank

octagon	parallelogram	pentagon
rectangle	rhombus	square
trapezoid	triangle	

1. I am a polygon with 4 sides. I have 2 pairs of parallel sides. My sides all have equal lengths. I have no right angles. What am I?

_____

2. I have an odd number of sides. I have more than 3 sides, but less than half a dozen. What am I?

_____

3. I am a polygon with 4 vertices. None of my sides form a right angle. I have one pair of parallel lines. What am I?

_____

4. I am a polygon. Sometimes, I am called by a more specific name such as *rhombus* or *rectangle*. I have 2 pairs of parallel sides. What am I?

_____

5. My sides are all equal. I only have right angles. What am I?

_____

6. I have all right angles and two pairs of equal, parallel sides. What am I?

_____

Write your own polygon riddles.

7. _____

_____

8. _____

_____

9. _____

_____

Quadrilaterals

A **quadrilateral** is a closed figure with four sides and four angles. Make four different quadrilaterals. Record your figures here.

1.

2.

3.

4.

What makes each of these figures a quadrilateral? _____

5.

a parallelogram that isn't a rectangle

6.

a parallelogram that is a square

7.

a quadrilateral that is a trapezoid

8.

a rectangle that is a square

9.

a rectangle that isn't a square

10.

a quadrilateral that isn't a trapezoid or parallelogram

11.

a parallelogram that is a rectangle

12.

a square that is a rectangle

13.

a trapezoid with only 1 right angle

14.

a quadrilateral that is not a parallelogram

15.

a quadrilateral with 4 right angles

16.

a quadrilateral with 4 equal sides

Quadrilateral Bump

Materials: 1 die, 10 two-color counters per player, 2 game pieces

To play: Players take turns. Roll the die and move your game piece that number of spaces on the game board. Read the name of the quadrilateral you land on and identify an example of it on the game board. Player 2 confirms whether player 1 has identified the correct type of quadrilateral. If correct, player 1 can cover that quadrilateral in the center of the game board. If incorrect, player 2 takes a turn. You can "bump" the other player off of a space if they only have 1 counter on it. Once you place 2 counters on a shape, it is yours and cannot be bumped. The first player to use all of his counters wins.

Start →	Choose any quadrilateral.	rhombus	trapezoid	rectangle	square
trapezoid					parallelogram
rhombus					Choose any quadrilateral.
Choose any quadrilateral.					rhombus
parallelogram					trapezoid
square					rectangle
rectangle	trapezoid	rhombus	Choose any quadrilateral.	parallelogram	square

Partitioning and Fractions

 Essential Question

What unit fractions can be used to define the equal parts of a shape?

 Warm-Up/Review

Draw a rectangle on the board, divided into fourths. Shade 1 part of the rectangle. Ask students, "What fraction of this rectangle is shaded?" (1/4) Ask them to explain how they know, and discuss with the class.

 Mini-Lesson

Materials: centimeter graph paper

1. Draw a 6 x 6 square on graph paper. Say, "Shapes can be partitioned into parts with equal areas. Each area is a fraction of the whole." Demonstrate how to partition the square into fourths and label each fourth 1/4.

2. Draw the 6 x 6 square on graph paper again. This time, divide the square into unequal fourths and label each 1/4. Ask, "Is this a correct way to partition the square? Why or why not?" Students should say no, because they are unequal parts.

3. Practice with other polygons. Have students draw the shapes and partition them into different amounts and label each section with a unit fraction.

4. Write the unit fraction 1/3. Have students draw any shape and partition and label it with 1/3. Ask students to share their drawings and discuss. Repeat with several more unit fractions.

 Math Talk

Is there more than one way to partition a shape? Explain.

Explain why it is important to be sure that each part is equal.

When would you need to partition something equally in the real world?

 Journal Prompt

Draw three rectangles. Partition each rectangle into fourths in a different way. Label each part with the appropriate fraction.

Materials

pre-cut circles, squares, and rectangles
pattern blocks

 Workstations

Activity sheets (pages 179–181)
Partitioning Three-in-a-Row
(page 182)

 Guided Math

⬤ Remediation: Hands-On Partitioning

1. Give each student a pre-cut circle. Say, "I want to partition this circle into halves. I can fold it in half to get two equal parts." Demonstrate how to fold the circle in half. Label each half *1/2*. Show students that you can turn the circle a different way to demonstrate how to partition the circle differently (vertically versus horizontally).

2. Explain that you can also partition the circle into fourths by folding the circle in half, and then in half again. Open it up and point out the 4 parts of the circle on the other side. Label each part with *1/4*.

3. Do the same thing with a pre-cut rectangle and a pre-cut square. Explain each time that by changing the orientation of the shape, you can partition it differently.

4. Have students follow along to fold and label the shapes as you model with yours.

▢ On Level: Partitioning with Pattern Blocks

1. Give each student a set of pattern blocks. Have each of them pull out a yellow hexagon. Say, "How many red trapezoids will make a yellow hexagon?" Students can use the red trapezoids to fit on top of the hexagon to show that 2 red trapezoids make a yellow hexagon. Ask, "What fraction of the hexagon is the trapezoid?" (1/2) Have students draw the hexagon, divide it in half, and label each half *1/2*.

2. Next ask, "How many green triangles make a hexagon?" Allow students time to explore and place the green triangles on top of the hexagon to determine how many will fit. Students should discover that 6 triangles make a hexagon. Ask, "What fraction is the triangle of the hexagon?" (1/6) Have students draw and label the divided hexagon.

3. Continue practicing with the rhombuses and the hexagon, the trapezoid and the triangles, and the rhombus and triangle, each time dividing and labeling the parts.

△ Enrichment: Real-World Partitioning

1. Share the following problem: *Austin has a rectangular candy bar. He has 2 friends and wants to share his candy bar with all of them. Draw a picture of the candy bar and show one way Austin can divide it equally with his friends. Label each part.*

2. Have students draw the candy bar and partition it. Observe to see if students are dividing the candy bar in halves or thirds. Explain that students should be dividing it into thirds because it is Austin and his 2 friends that are sharing the candy bar. Have students show another way that Austin can divide the candy bar that is different from the first way they drew.

3. Share more real-world instances where students would have to partition something, and have them draw how they would solve it.

 Assess and Extend

Have students solve the following problem: *Brittany is planting a flower garden in a square-shaped bed. She wants to plant daisies, tulips, daffodils, and lilies. She must give each flower an equal amount of space in the garden. Draw a diagram that shows how Brittany's garden can be divided in a way that will give all the flowers an equal amount of space.*

Name _____   Date _____

 Partitioning and Fractions   Hands-On Partitioning

Partition each shape. Shade and label it to show the fraction given.

1.  $\dfrac{1}{4}$	**2.** 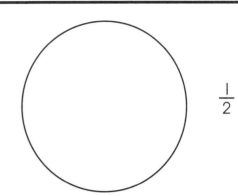 $\dfrac{1}{2}$
3. 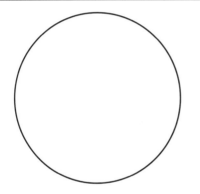 $\dfrac{1}{4}$	**4.** 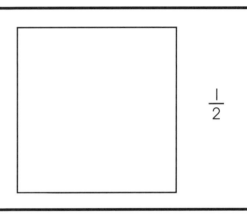 $\dfrac{1}{2}$
5. 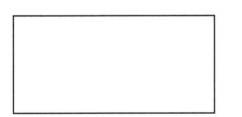 $\dfrac{1}{6}$	**6.** 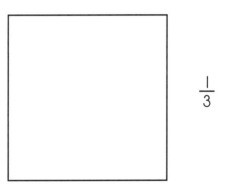 $\dfrac{1}{3}$
7. 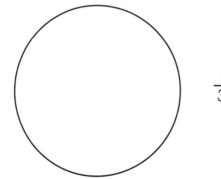 $\dfrac{1}{3}$	**8.** 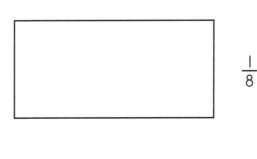 $\dfrac{1}{8}$

Partitioning and Fractions   ☐ Partitioning with Pattern Blocks

Tell how each shape is partitioned.

1. 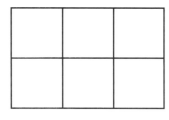   2. 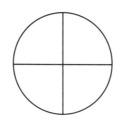   3.

_____   _____   _____

4. Partition each shape as given. Then, label each part with the appropriate fraction.

halves	sixths	eighths
sixths	halves	fourths
fifths	thirds	fifths

Name _____   Date _____

 Partitioning and Fractions   ▲ Real-World Partitioning

Solve. Draw a picture to show your work.

1. Charlotte made brownies in a rectangular pan to share with 5 of her friends. Show how Charlotte can divide the brownies so that she and each of her friends gets the same size brownie.

2. A home builder needs 10 pieces of wood to finish a project in one of his houses. He has 1 large piece of wood in the shape of a rectangle that he can use. Show how the home builder would need to cut the piece of wood in order to have enough to finish his project.

3. Dave ordered a large, round pepperoni pizza. His pizza must feed his family of 8. How can Dave divide up the pizza so that everyone gets 1 slice of pizza?

4. Mrs. Walker bought a large chocolate chip cookie cake for her son's birthday. Her son invited 3 friends over to celebrate his birthday. How can Mrs. Walker divide up the cookie cake so that her son and his 3 friends each get the same amount of the chocolate chip cookie cake?

5. Leslie made a lemon cake for her neighbor. She baked it in a square baking pan. If Leslie wants to keep half of the lemon cake for herself, how can she divide the cake so that she can keep half and give the other half to her neighbor?

Partitioning Three-in-a-Row

Materials: two-color counters, paper clip, sharpened pencil

To play: Players take turns. Use a sharpened pencil and a paper clip to spin the spinner. Place your counter on a shape on the board that has the matching amount partitioned. If a counter is already on a space, you may not place a counter on the same space. The first player with three counters in a row wins.

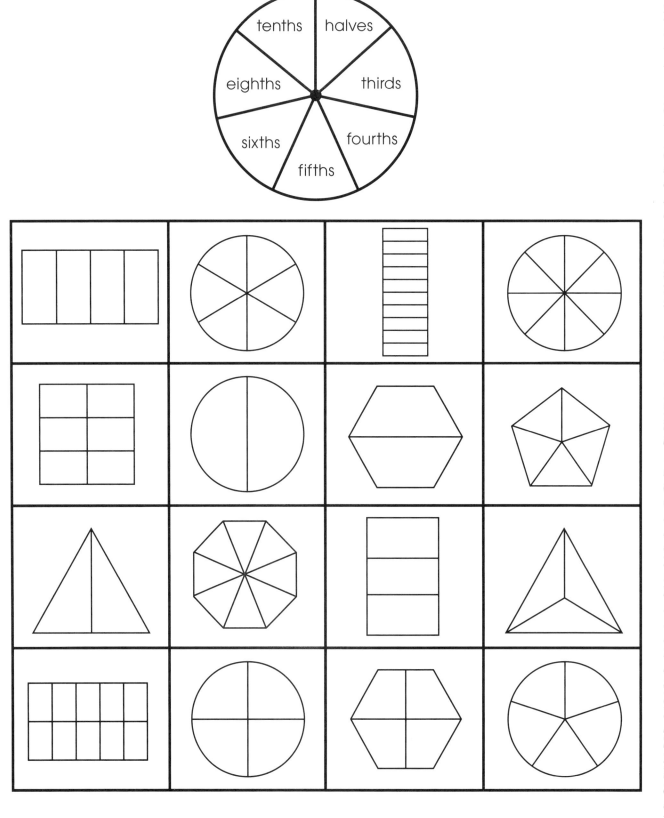

Name _____   Date _____

ten thousands	thousands	hundreds	tens	ones

Word Form

Expanded Form

Number *of the Day*

Write an addition or subtraction sentence using the number. Solve.

What number is	
−100	+100
−1,000	+1,000

Round to the nearest

ten _____

hundred _____

Fraction *of the Day*

shaded parts ☐

equal parts in all ☐

Model it.

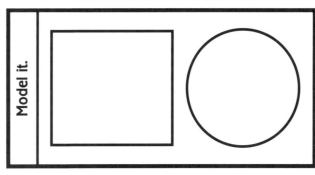

Place it on a number line.

⟵———————————————⟶

Name an equivalent fraction.

Show it on the number line.

☐/☐

This fraction is

☐ greater than

☐ equal to

☐ less than

$\dfrac{1}{2}$.

Use >, <, or = to compare.

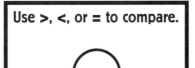

What fraction is needed to reach the next whole number?

_____ + _____ = _____

Materials: 2 dice, 10 counters (in two colors) per player

To play: Players take turns. Roll the dice and _____ .
Cover the answer. You can "bump" the other player off of a space if there is only one counter on it. Once you place two counters on a space, it is yours and cannot be bumped. The player to use all of his or her counters first wins.

BUMP!

To prep: Complete the title with the skill. Fill in the spaces with possible answers. Complete the directions with instructions related to the skill that describe how students use the numbers they roll. For example, *multiply the numbers* or *add, then cover the number that is two less.* Cut these directions off before copying. If desired, copy on cardstock and laminate for durability. Place it in a station with the related materials.

_____ Four-in-a-Row

Materials: _____ dice, two different colors of counters

To play: Players take turns. _____
_____ . Place your counter on
the answer. If a counter is already on a space, you may not place a counter on the same
space. The first player with four counters in a row wins.

○ ○ ○ ○ ○ ○

○ ○ ○ ○ ○ ○

○ ○ ○ ○ ○ ○

○ ○ ○ ○ ○ ○

○ ○ ○ ○ ○ ○

○ ○ ○ ○ ○ ○

- ✂

To prep: Fill in the circles with numbers. Place the numbers in random order and repeat numbers throughout.
Fill in the number of dice needed in the Materials section. Complete the directions with instructions specific to
the skill. For example, *roll two dice and add the numbers,* or *roll three dice, place the numbers in any order to
create a three-digit number, and round it to the nearest ten.* Cut off these directions before copying. If desired,
copy it on cardstock and laminate for durability. Place it in a station with the related materials.

Path Game

Materials: I die, I game piece for each player

To play: Players take turns. Roll the die. Move forward that many spaces. Solve the problem or follow the instructions on the space. If using cards, draw a card and solve the problem. If you answer correctly, stay on the space. If you answer incorrectly, return to your previous space. The first player to reach the Finish space wins.

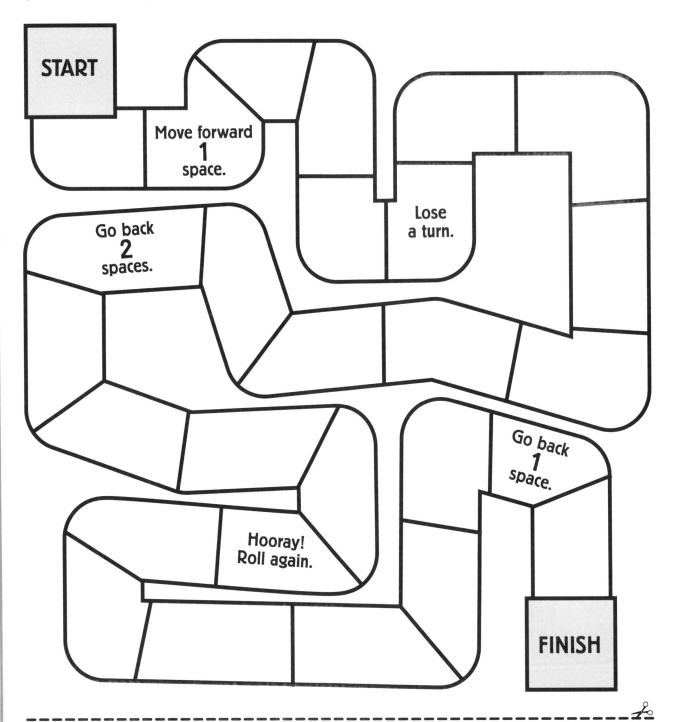

To prep: Fill in the title with a fun or skill-based name. If using cards, add them to the materials list and create cards with problems or prompts on cardstock or index cards. If not using cards, write problems directly on the blank spaces. Cut off these directions before copying. If desired, copy them on cardstock and laminate for durability. Place them in a station with the related materials.

_____ Roll and Solve

Materials: I die

To play: Roll the die. Find the matching column and solve the bottom problem. Continue rolling and solving the next problem in each column until one column is complete. Color the winning animal. Continue to see which animals win second and third place.

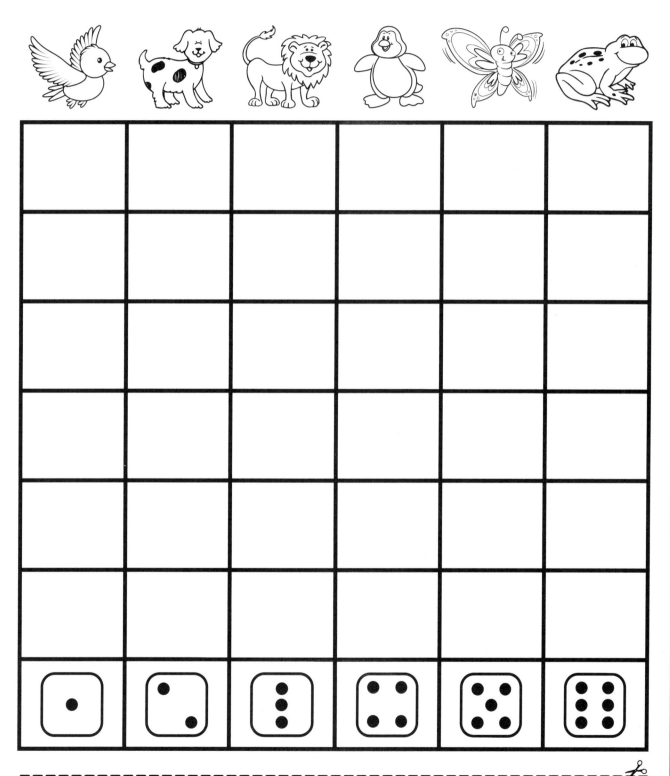

- ✂

To prep: Complete the title with the skill. Fill in the spaces below each animal with different problems. Cut off these directions before copying. If desired, copy them on cardstock and laminate for durability. Place them in a station with the related materials.

_____ Flip!

To play: Shuffle the cards. Place them all facedown. Players take turns. The first player flips over one card and _____
_____. If the player answers correctly, he may keep the card. If not, return the card facedown to the pile. Once all of the cards have been flipped, the player with the most cards wins.

- ✂

To prep: Complete the title with the skill. Fill in the cards with numbers or other prompts, such as geometric figures, angles, or shapes. Complete the directions by telling how students should answer or solve the prompts on the cards. For example, _tell what type of angle is shown,_ or _tell how many to add to make 10._ Copy the cards on cardstock for durability and laminate if desired. Place them in a center with the directions. You may include a spatula and paper plates with the activity for students to use when "flipping" the cards and maintaining their "keep" piles.

Shut the Box

_____ **Shut the Box**

Materials: _____ dice, _____ counters per person

To play: Cover all of the spaces on your board with counters. Players take turns. Roll the dice. _____
_____ If
it has already been uncovered, mark one of your strikes. After one player has gotten three strikes, the player who has removed the most counters wins. Or, the first player to remove all of the counters without getting three strikes wins.

Player 1

Strike ① ② ③

Strike ① ② ③

Player 2

- ✂

To prep: Complete the title with the skill. Fill in the spaces on each section with the possible answers. Both sections should have the same numbers. You do not have to fill in all of the spaces. Complete the materials section with the number of dice and counters needed. Complete the directions with instructions related to the skill that describe how students use the numbers they roll. For example, *double the number, then uncover the answer,* or *add, then uncover the sum.* Cut off these directions before copying. If desired, copy them on cardstock and laminate for durability. Place them in a station with the related materials.

Answer Key

Page 17
1. 2 + 2 + 2 + 2 = 8, 4, 2, 8, 4 × 2 = 8;
2. 4 + 4 + 4 = 12, 3, 4, 12, 3 × 4 = 12;
3. 5 + 5 + 5 + 5 + 5 = 25, 5, 5, 25,
5 × 5 = 25; 4. 3 + 3 + 3 + 3 + 3
+ 3 = 18, 6, 3, 18, 6 × 3 = 18; 5. 6,
3 + 3 = 6, 2 × 3 = 6; 6. 20, 5 + 5 +
5 + 5 = 20, 4 × 5 = 20; Check
students' work.

Page 18
1–6. Answers will vary.

Page 19
Check students' work. 1. 10 + 10,
20; 2. 15 + 15 + 15 + 15, 60;
3. 12 + 12, 24; 4. 14 + 14 + 14, 42;
5. 10 + 10 + 10 + 10 + 10 + 10, 60;
6. 11 + 11 + 11, 33; 7. 13 + 13 + 13 +
13, 52; 8. 0; 9. 20 + 20 + 20 + 20, 80;
10. 12 + 12 + 12 + 12 + 12, 60; 11. 10
+ 10 + 10 + 10 + 10, 50; 12. 13 + 13,
26; 13. 14; 14. 11 + 11, 22

Page 23
Check students' work. 1. 12 ÷ 3 = 4;
2. 8 ÷ 4 = 2; 3. 24 ÷ 3 = 8;
4. 12 ÷ 4 = 3; 5. 9 ÷ 3 = 3;
6. 5 ÷ 1 = 5; 7. 10 ÷ 5 = 2;
8. 25 ÷ 5 = 5; 9. 12 ÷ 6 = 2;
10. 16 ÷ 4 = 4

Page 24
Check students' work. 1. 9, 9; 2. 6,
6; 3. 4, 4; 4. 9, 9; 5. 8, 8; 6. 9, 9; 7. 4,
4; 8. 4, 4; 9. 5, 5; 10. 4, 4; 11. 5, 5;
12. 9, 9; 13. 6, 6; 14. 5, 5

Page 25
1. ÷10; 2. ÷5, 6, 20; 3. ÷2, 8, 10;
4. ÷3, 8, 27; 5. ÷7, 5, 56; 6. ÷4, 12, 36;
7–8. Answers will vary.

Page 29
Multiplication sentences will vary.
1. 2; 2. 6; 3. 8; 4. 6; 5. 8; 6. 5; 7. 9;
8. 3; 9. 5; 10. 5; 11. 4; 12. 2; 13. 3;
14. 4; 15. 9; 16. 9; 17. 7; 18. 9; 19. 8;
20. 7; 21. 8; 22. 5; 23. 3; 24. 3

Page 30
Related multiplication facts will
vary. 1. 14; 2. 3; 3. 18; 4. 3; 5. 3;
6. 18; 7. 4; 8. 24; 9. 15; 10. 4; 11. 2;
12. 56; 13. 2; 14. 8; 15. 36

Page 31
Check all fact families. 1. 27; 2. 3;
3. 8; 4. 6; 5. 72; 6. 4; 7. 4; 8. 40; 9. 6;
10. 7; 11. 30; 12. 7; 13. 6; 14. 64; 15. 9

Page 35
Check students' work. 1. 3; 2. 6;
3. 5; 4. 2; 5. 9; 6. 2; 7. 2; 8. 2; 9. 3;
10. 4; 11. 18; 12. 32

Page 36
1. 4; 2. 4; 3. 5; 4. 2; 5. 24; 6. 36; 7. 3;
8. 5; 9. 8; 10. 6; 11. 8; 12. 8; 13. 5;
14. 9; 15. 12; 16. 7; 17. 4; 18. 9; 19. 6;
20. 15; 21. 7

Page 37
Multiplication and division
problems will vary. 1. 7; 2. 6; 3. 20;
4. 32; 5. 2; 6. 9; 7. 9; 8. 12; 9. 8;
10. 36; 11. 6; 12. 6

Page 41
Check students' work. 1. 120
cookies; 2. 9 slices; 3. 47 miles;
4. 37 pages; 5. 91 insects;
6. 5 flowers

Page 42
Check students' work. 1. 8 more
balloons; 2. 32 more cans and
boxes; 3. 54 apples; 4. $10;
5. 8 times; 6. 24 clean pages

Page 43
Answers will vary.

Page 44
A. $1.23; B. 42 pieces; C. Ivan;
D. 88 pencils and erasers;
E. 4 turtles and 5 snails;
F. 119 hours; G. 6 cupcakes;
H. 104 crayons

Page 47
1. +10; 2. –5; 3. +9; 4. +7; 5. –3; 6. ×2

Page 48
1. –10; 2. +15, 185, 395; 3. ×6, 48, 66;
4. +25, 270, 950; 5. times itself, 36,
64; 6. +150, 390, 450; 7–8. Answers
will vary.

Page 49
1. –150, 650, 350; 2. ×2, 136, 80;
3. ×3, 225, 105; 4. ×10, +2; 702;
5. ×5, +1; 31, 41; 6. ÷2, 500, 100;
7–8. Answers will vary.

Page 50
train: +7; 27, 62; alligator: add
double the previous amount;
77; ship: subtract 1 less than the
previous amount; 795, 753

Page 53
1. tens, 30; 2. ones, 7; 3. hundreds,
700; 4. thousands, 6,000; 5.
hundreds, 500; 6. hundreds, 400;
7. hundreds, 200; 8. tens, 40;
9. ones, 1; 10. thousands, 8,000;
11. 900 + 70 + 1; 12. 2,000 + 100 +
40 + 5; 13. 80 + 6; 14. 6,000 + 200 +
30; 15. 900 + 50 + 2; 16. 743; 17. 512;
18. 76; 19. 1,430; 20. 3,637

Page 54
1. thousands, 5,000; 2. hundreds,
100; 3. ones, 4; 4. hundred
thousands, 300,000; 5. hundreds,
200; 6. tens, 80; 7. ten thousands,
90,000; 8. ones, 8; 9. thousands,
2,000; 10. tens, 0; 11. 5,000 + 800 +
90 + 7; 12. 2,000 + 300 + 8;
13. 70,000 + 6,000 + 400 + 50;
14. 7,000 + 800 + 70 + 6; 15. 200,000
+ 20,000 + 4,000 + 300 + 40 + 1;
16. 421,361; 17. 4,681; 18. 3,523;
19. 685,510; 20. 4,735

Page 55
1. tens, 0; 2. hundreds, 100;
3. ones, 4; 4. thousands, 9,000;
5. ten thousands, 90,000; 6. 30,000
+ 8,000 + 800 + 10 + 2; 7. 600,000 +
70,000 + 8,000 + 900 + 30 + 3;
8. 50,000 + 9,000 + 4; 9. 40,000 +
40 + 5; 10. 9,000,000 + 700,000 +
30,000 + 3,000 + 300 + 10 + 2;
11. 34,753; 12. 63,471; 13. 2,734,501;
14. 50,027; 15. 67,274; 16. 55,345;
17. 97,432; 18. 940; 19. 67,000;
20. 85,400

Page 59
1. 20; 2. 80; 3. 40; 4. 10; 5. 40; 6. 90;
7. 50; 8. 40; 9. 100; 10. 60; 11. 200;
12. 900; 13. 800; 14. 600; 15. 100;
16. 700; 17. 300; 18. 800; 19. 600;
20. 900

Page 60
1. 200; 2. 800; 3. 900; 4. 200; 5. 200;
6. 500; 7. 400; 8. 500; 9. 400;
10. 400; 11. 2,000; 12. 9,000;
13. 5,000; 14. 6,000; 15. 8,000;
16. 2,000; 17. 6,000; 18. 4,000;
19. 7,000; 20. 10,000

Page 61
1. 20, tens; 2. 15,000, thousands;
3. 8,000, thousands; 4. 300,
hundreds; 5. 70,000, ten

Answer Key

thousands; 6. 73,980, tens; 7. 90, tens; 8. 40,000, ten thousands; 9. 600, hundreds; 10. 4,620, tens; 11. 70, tens; 12. 500, hundreds; 13. 10,000, thousands; 14. 600, tens; 15. 7,000, thousands; 16. 82,000, thousands; 17. 240, tens; 18. 3,000, hundreds; 19. 50,000, ten thousands; 20. 720, tens

Page 65
1. 90; 2. 81; 3. 73; 4. 60; 5. 82; 6. 70; 7. 75; 8. 77; 9. 57; 10. 83; 11. 74; 12. 80; 13. 95; 14. 99; 15. 90; 16. 85; 17. 47; 18. 81; 19. 67; 20. 40

Page 66
1. 561; 2. 811; 3. 953; 4. 740; 5. 242; 6. 700; 7. 815; 8. 568; 9. 820; 10. 832; 11. 5,382; 12. 9,600; 13. 9,507; 14. 9,019; 15. 6,510; 16. 5,219; 17. 8,144; 18. 9,665; 19. 8,029; 20. 8,961

Page 67
1. 7,443, didn't regroup to the tens or the hundreds places; 2. 9,773, didn't regroup to the hundreds place; 3. correct; 4. 100,760, didn't regroup to the tens or the ten thousands places; 5. 61,089, didn't regroup to the thousands place; 6. correct; 7. 50,092, didn't regroup to the thousands or the ten thousands places; 8. 96,246, didn't regroup to the hundreds or the thousands places; 9. correct; 10. 61,990, didn't regroup to the tens or the ten thousands places

Page 71
1. 26; 2. 11; 3. 65; 4. 8; 5. 8; 6. 17; 7. 11; 8. 55; 9. 19; 10. 4; 11. 33; 12. 12; 13. 14; 14. 3; 15. 46; 16. 12; 17. 11; 18. 30; 19. 57; 20. 38

Page 72
1. 12; 2. 68; 3. 29; 4. 45; 5. 24; 6. 377; 7. 376; 8. 532; 9. 286; 10. 450; 11. 4,600; 12. 5,958; 13. 1,757; 14. 1,976; 15. 8,591; 16. 579

Page 73
Estimates will vary. 1. 204; 2. 359; 3. 705; 4. 155; 5. 2,772; 6. 1,150; 7. 960; 8. 2,273; 9. 19,146; 10. 55,957; 11. 25,784; 12. 9,106; 13. 49,957; 14. 25,556; 15. 50,577

Page 77
Check students' work. 1. 120; 2. 80; 3. 120; 4. 180; 5. 360; 6. 210; 7. 200; 8. 240; 9. 560; 10. 250; 11. 120; 12. 240; 13. 90; 14. 210; 15. 120; 16. 210

Page 78
1. 270; 2. 630; 3. 320; 4. 480; 5. 350; 6. 150; 7. 360; 8. 240; 9. 350; 10. 150; 11. 320; 12. 80; 13. 270; 14. 30; 15. 40; 16. 720

Page 79
1. 4,500; 2. 5,400; 3. 3,200; 4. 2,000; 5. 2,100; 6. 1,800; 7. 1,200; 8. 3,600; 9. 3,000; 10. 4,000; 11. 2,800; 12. 4,900; 13. 2,400; 14. 7,200; 15. 660; 16. 820

Page 83
1. 1/3; 2. 3/6; 3. 1/4; 4. 1/4; 5. 1/2; 6. 2/4; 7. 4/8; 8. 1/3; 9. 1/2; 10. 2/3; 11. 1/2; 12. 3/12

Page 84
Check students' work.

Page 85
1. 1/4; 2. 2/6; 3. 3/4; 4. 6/12; 5. 5/15; 6. 4/8; 7. 4/4; 8. 2/10; 9. 2/12; 10. 12/16; 11–16. Check students' work.

Page 89
1. 5; 2. Check students' work. 3. 1/5; 4. Check students' work. 5. 8; 6. Check students' work. 7. 1/8; 8. Check students' work. 9. 10; 10. Check students' work. 11. 1/10; 12. Check students' work.

Page 90
1. A. 1/2; B. 1/3; C. 2/3; D. 1/4; E. 2/4; F. 3/4; G. 1/6; H. 2/6; I. 3/6; J. 4/6; K. 5/6; 2. B; 3. D; 4. J; 5. A; 6. H; 7. F; 8. Answers will vary. Check students' work.

Page 91
Check students' work.

Page 92
A. 1/2; B. 1/4; C. 3/4; D. 4/5; E. 4/6; F. 3/8; G. 2/7; H. 1/5; I. 2/6; J. 1/3; K. 3/8; L. 2/7

Page 95
1. 1/3, 2/6; 2. 1/4, 2/8; 3. 1/2, 3/6; 4. 3/4, 6/8; 5. 2/2, 1/1; 6. 1/3, 2/6; 7. 2/3, 6/9; 8. 2/3, 4/6; 9. 8/8, 1/1; 10. 2/4; 11. 1/4; 12. 1/4; 13. 1/2;

14. 6/8; 15. 3/4; Check students' work.

Page 96
1. 2/3, 4/6; 2. 2/4, 4/8; 3. 1/4, 2/8; 4. 2; 5. 2; 6. 6; 7. 6; 8. 6; 9. 2; 10. 3; 11. 3; 12. 2; 13. 2; 14–15. Answers will vary.

Page 97
Check students' work. X: 1, 2, 6, 7

Page 101
1. 3/3; 2. 8/8; 3. 2/2; 4. 6/6; 5. 1; 6. 1; 7. 1; 8. 1; 9–10. All parts of the shape should be shaded.

Page 102
Check students' work. 1. 2/2, 4/2, 6/2, 8/2; 2. 4/4, 8/4, 12/4, 16/4; 3. 6/6, 12/6, 18/6, 24/6; 4. 8/8, 16/8, 24/8, 32/8

Page 103
Check students' work. 1. 3 1/4; 2. 2 2/4; 3. 2 2/8; 4. 4 1/5; 5. 2 1/7; 6. 3 5/6; 7. 2 1/3; 8. 3 1/6; 9. 1 8/9; 10. 4 1/2; 11. 9 3/4; 12. 2 3/6

Page 107
1. 1/3 < 2/3; 2. 2/8 < 4/8; 3. 3/8 < 3/4; 4. 2/4 > 2/6; 5. 3/4 > 2/4; 6. 1/2 = 1/2; 7. 6/8 = 3/4; 8. 5/6 > 5/10

Page 108
1. 1/5 > 1/2, <; 1/6 > 1/3, >; 2. 2/5 > 4/5, <; 4/8 > 6/8, <; 3. 1/2 < 1/4, >; 5/6 < 2/6, >; 5/6 < 5/12, >; 4. 2/9 > 3/9, <; 2/9 > 4/9, <; 5. 1/3 < 1/6, >; 6. 1/5 > 1/3, <; 5/6 < 3/6, >

Page 109
1. >; 2. <; 3. <; 4. <; 5. <; 6. >; 7. =; 8. >; 9. <; 10. <; 11. <; 12. <; 13. >; 14. =; 15. >; 16. >; 17. =; 18. <

Page 113
1. 3:00; 2. 7:17; 3. 12:45; 4. 2:46; 5. 2:08; 6. 10:30; 7. 6:33; 8. 6:45; 9. 1:51; 10. 9:30; 11. 12:28; 12. 10:45; 13. 10:44; 14. 3:18; 15. 8:12; 16. 4:39

Page 114
Check students' work.

Page 115
Check students' work.

Page 119
1. 11; 2. 4; 3. 2; 4. 5; 5. 2; 6. 3

Answer Key

Page 120
1. 32 min.; 2. 1 hr. 19 min.;
3. 32 min.; 4. 7:04; 5. 4:29; 6. 5:33;
7. 40 min.; 8. 8:55; 9. 16 min.;
10. 3:05

Page 121
Check students' work.

Page 125
1. g; 2. g; 3. g; 4. g; 5. kg; 6. g; 7. kg;
8. g; 9. 100 g; 10. 9 g

Page 126
1. 6 kg; 2. 324 kg; 3. 15 kg;
4. 60 bouncy balls; 5. 54 kg;
6. 740 g; 7. 48 g

Page 127
1. kg; 2. g; 3. g; 4. kg; 5. g; 6. kg;
7. g; 8. kg; 9. $400; 10. 459 g; 11.
346 kg; 12. 50 kg; 13. 745 g

Page 131
1. mL; 2. mL; 3. mL; 4. L; 5. mL; 6. L;
7. mL; 8. L; 9. 18 L; 10. 1,200 mL

Page 132
1. 84 L; 2. 303 mL; 3. 13 L, 14 mL
wouldn't be enough for a party;
4. 160 L; 5. No, because there are
only 94 mL left. 6. 645 mL; 7. 30 L

Page 133
1. 56 mL; 2. 94 mL; 3. 24 mL;
4. 16 mL; 5. 76 mL; 6. 52 mL;
7. 31 mL; 8. 38 mL; 9. 47 mL

Page 134
A. kg; B. L; C. g; D. g; E. 17 L;
F. 945 g; G. 72 mL; H. 4 L; I. 350 mL;
J. 700 mL; K. 500 mL; L. 4 L

Page 137
Check students' graphs. 1.
7 students; 2. pizza; 3. grilled
cheese; 4. 25 students; 5. 4
students; 6. swimming; 7. 9
students; 8. tennis

Page 138
Check students' work. 1. 5th; 2. 1st,
4th; 3. 125 students; 4. Answers will
vary. 5. September; 6. 1,700 tickets;
7–8. Answers will vary.

Page 139
Answers will vary.

Page 143
1. 7 students; 2. 7 years old;
3. 8 years old; 4. 13 students;
5. 0 points; 6. 6 students;
7. 5 students; 8. 20 students

Page 144
Answers will vary.

Page 145
Answers will vary.

Page 146
A. 6 crayons; B. 12 fish;
C. 12 paintbrushes; D. 4 more
sticks; E–J. Check students' work.

Page 149
1. 24 sq. units; 2. 63 sq. units;
3. 48 sq. units; 4. 50 sq. units;
5. 16 sq. units; 6. 18 sq. units;
7. 56 sq. units; 8. 40 sq. units;
9. 66 sq. units; 10. 35 sq. units;
11. 25 sq. units; 12. 54 sq. units;
13. 28 sq. units; 14. 42 sq. units;
15. 12 sq. units

Page 150
1. 9 sq. units; 2. 12 sq. units;
3. 20 sq. units; 4. 12 sq. units;
5. 12 sq. units; 6. 9 sq. units;
7. 30 sq. units; 8. 15 sq. units;
9. 8 sq. units; 10. 2 sq. units

Page 151
1. 63 sq. ft.; 2. 88 sq. ft.;
3. 480 sq. m; 4. 100 sq. ft.;
5. 560 sq. m; 6. 30 sq. m; 7. 120 tiles

Page 155
1. 15 sq. in.; 2. 16 sq. ft.;
3. 16 sq. ft.; 4. 49 sq. in.;
5. 45 sq. in.; 6. 30 sq. yd.;
7. 9 sq. m; 8. 14 sq. cm;
9. 60 sq. mm; 10. 70 sq. cm;
11. 80 sq. mm; 12. 25 sq. mm

Page 156
1. 16 tiles; 2. 180 sq. m; 3. 90 sq. ft.;
4. 90 sq. yd.; 5. 30 sq. m;
6. 56 sq. ft.; 7. 30 sq. ft.;
Challenge: 9 ft.

Page 157
Division problems will vary. 1. 5 cm;
2. 2 cm; 3. 3 ft.; 4. 4 in.; 5. 10 ft.;
6. 3 cm; 7. 8 in.; 8. 8 cm; 9. 9 m

Page 161
1. 28; 2. 32; 3. 25; 4. 27; 5. 20; 6. 32;
7. 21; 8. 12; 9. 26; 10. 24; 11. 21; 12. 11

Page 162
1. 67 sq. ft.; 2. 75 sq. m;
3. 5 sq. units; 4. 16 sq. cm;
5. 44 sq. m; 6. 28 sq. mi.

Page 163
1. 31 sq. in., 36 – 5 = 31; 2. 33 sq. m,
48 – 15 = 33; 3. 48 sq. m,
64 – 16 = 48; 4. 5 sq. in., 6 – 1 = 5;
5. 84 sq. mi., 100 – 16 = 84;
6. 75 sq. km, 90 – 15 = 75;
7. 34 sq. m, Answers will vary but
may include 70 – 36 = 34.
8. 80 sq. in., Answers will vary but
may include 144 – 64 = 80.

Page 167
1. 10; 2. 18; 3. 14; 4. 16; 5. 12; 6. 12;
7. 22; 8. 24

Page 168
1. Students should draw
rectangles with the following
dimensions: 1 × 11, 2 × 10, 3 × 9,
4 × 8, 5 × 7, 6 × 6; 2. Students
should draw rectangles with the
following dimensions: 1 × 14,
2 × 13, 3 × 12, 4 × 11, 5 × 10, 6 × 9,
7 × 8; 3. 16 cm; 4. 26 mm; 5. 12 in.;
6. 28 ft.

Page 169
1. 10 cm; 2. 14 in.; 3. 16 in.; 4. 11 ft.;
5. 16 m; 6. 14 cm; 7. 12 yd.; 8. 14 ft.;
9. 18 in.

Page 170
A. 42 mm; B. 26 in.; C. 18 ft.;
D. 24 mm; E. 11 in.; F. 18 mm;
G. 12 ft.; H. 12 cm; I. 35 mm;
J. 52 in.; K. 9 cm; L. 10 ft.

Page 173
1. square; 2. rectangle;
3. trapezoid; 4. parallelogram;
5. rhombus; 6. rectangle;
7. square; 8. trapezoid;
9. parallelogram

Page 174
1. rhombus; 2. pentagon;
3. trapezoid; 4. parallelogram;
5. square; 6. rectangle;
7–9. Answers will vary.

Page 175
Check students' work. Drawings
will vary.

Page 179
Check students' work.

Page 180
1. sixths; 2. fourths; 3. thirds;
4. Check students' work.

Page 181
Answers will vary.